BY ROBERT D. KAPLAN

WASTE LAND: A WORLD IN PERMANENT CRISIS

THE LOOM OF TIME: BETWEEN EMPIRE AND ANARCHY,
FROM THE MEDITERRANEAN TO CHINA

THE TRAGIC MIND: FEAR, FATE, AND THE BURDEN OF POWER

ADRIATIC: A CONCERT OF CIVILIZATIONS AT THE END OF THE MODERN AGE

THE GOOD AMERICAN: THE EPIC LIFE OF BOB GERSONY,
THE U.S. GOVERNMENT'S GREATEST HUMANITARIAN

THE RETURN OF MARCO POLO'S WORLD: WAR, STRATEGY,
AND AMERICAN INTERESTS IN THE TWENTY-FIRST CENTURY

EARNING THE ROCKIES: HOW GEOGRAPHY SHAPES
AMERICA'S ROLE IN THE WORLD

IN EUROPE'S SHADOW: TWO COLD WARS AND A
THIRTY-YEAR JOURNEY THROUGH ROMANIA AND BEYOND

ASIA'S CAULDRON: THE SOUTH CHINA SEA AND THE END OF A STABLE PACIFIC

THE REVENGE OF GEOGRAPHY: WHAT THE MAP TELLS US
ABOUT COMING CONFLICTS AND THE BATTLE AGAINST FATE

MONSOON: THE INDIAN OCEAN AND THE FUTURE OF AMERICAN POWER

HOG PILOTS, BLUE WATER GRUNTS: THE AMERICAN MILITARY IN
THE AIR, AT SEA, AND ON THE GROUND

IMPERIAL GRUNTS: THE AMERICAN MILITARY ON THE GROUND

MEDITERRANEAN WINTER: THE PLEASURES OF HISTORY AND LANDSCAPE
IN TUNISIA, SICILY, DALMATIA, AND THE PELOPONNESE

WARRIOR POLITICS: WHY LEADERSHIP DEMANDS A PAGAN ETHOS

EASTWARD TO TARTARY: TRAVELS IN THE BALKANS, THE MIDDLE EAST,
AND THE CAUCASUS

THE COMING ANARCHY: SHATTERING THE DREAMS OF THE POST COLD WAR

AN EMPIRE WILDERNESS: TRAVELS INTO AMERICA'S FUTURE

THE ENDS OF THE EARTH: FROM TOGO TO TURKMENISTAN,
FROM IRAN TO CAMBODIA

THE ARABISTS: THE ROMANCE OF AN AMERICAN ELITE

BALKAN GHOSTS: A JOURNEY THROUGH HISTORY

SOLDIERS OF GOD: WITH ISLAMIC WARRIORS IN AFGHANISTAN AND PAKISTAN

SURRENDER OR STARVE: TRAVELS IN ETHIOPIA, SUDAN, SOMALIA, AND ERITREA

WASTE LAND

WASTE LAND

A WORLD IN PERMANENT CRISIS

ROBERT D. KAPLAN

RANDOM HOUSE
NEW YORK

Copyright © 2025 by Robert D. Kaplan

Penguin Random House values and supports copyright. Copyright fuels creativity, encourages diverse voices, promotes free speech, and creates a vibrant culture. Thank you for buying an authorized edition of this book and for complying with copyright laws by not reproducing, scanning, or distributing any part of it in any form without permission. You are supporting writers and allowing Penguin Random House to continue to publish books for every reader. Please note that no part of this book may be used or reproduced in any manner for the purpose of training artificial intelligence technologies or systems.

Published in the United States by Random House, an imprint and division of Penguin Random House LLC, New York.

RANDOM HOUSE and the HOUSE colophon are registered trademarks of Penguin Random House LLC.

LIBRARY OF CONGRESS CATALOGING-IN-PUBLICATION DATA
NAMES: Kaplan, Robert D., author.
TITLE: Waste land / By Robert D. Kaplan.
DESCRIPTION: First edition. | New York, NY: Random House, [2025] | Includes index.
IDENTIFIERS: LCCN 2024034855 (print) | LCCN 2024034856 (ebook) | ISBN 9780593730324 (hardcover) | ISBN 9780593730348 (ebook)
SUBJECTS: LCSH: Geopolitics. | Power (Social sciences)—History. | Globalization—History. | International relations—History.
CLASSIFICATION: LCC JC319 .K336 2025 (print) | LCC JC319 (ebook) | DDC 320.1/2—dc23/eng/20240802
LC record available at https://lccn.loc.gov/2024034855
LC ebook record available at https://lccn.loc.gov/2024034856

Printed in the United States of America on acid-free paper

randomhousebooks.com

1st Printing

FIRST EDITION

Title-page art from Adobe Stock, Inset: Sofiia, and large image: zef art
Book design by Barbara M. Bachman

To Devon Cross

. . . hope, detached from faith and untempered by the evidence of history, is a dangerous asset, and one that threatens not only those who embrace it, but all those within range of their illusions.

—ROGER SCRUTON
The Uses of Pessimism

CONTENTS

**I.
WEIMAR GOES GLOBAL** *3*

**II.
THE GREAT POWERS IN DECLINE** *69*

**III.
CROWDS AND CHAOS** *129*

ACKNOWLEDGMENTS *187*

NOTES *189*

INDEX *197*

WASTE LAND

I.

WEIMAR GOES GLOBAL

PREMONITIONS CAN BE PRECIOUS. THEY OFFER AN UNCANNY, decipherable warning about something or other, especially if the person having them is at the right place at the right time. Consider the Anglo-American Christopher Isherwood and the German Alfred Döblin, novelists who each wrote about Berlin in the 1920s and early 1930s. In the guise of fiction, a writer can more easily tell the truth, hiding behind his characters and other forms of make-believe. Their Berlin is a fantastic, neurotic nightmare.

Isherwood, in *Goodbye to Berlin,* describes an edgy, decadent demimonde; marked by wholesale perversion and end-of-the-world partying; flaky characters on unending sprees of drinking and carousing all set against the backdrop of a "bankrupt middle class" living amid secondhand furniture in shabby, leaking buildings plastered with hammers-and-sickles and swastikas. He zooms in on a down-at-heel innkeeper, cleaning chamber pots, battered by the Great War and inflation. There are bank closures, sullen crowds, and the eerie pageant of burying social democracy amid black banners of one extremist group or the other. "Berlin is a skeleton which aches in the cold," Isherwood writes. "This town is sick with Jews. Turn over any stone, and a couple of them will crawl out. They're poisoning the very water we drink!" exclaims one of his characters.[1]

Isherwood lived in Berlin from 1929 to 1933, the year Adolf Hitler came to power, so *Goodbye to Berlin,* as prescient as the author's initial experiences were, was helped a bit by hindsight. Döblin's *Berlin Alexanderplatz* was published in the fall of 1929, when people had still not given up on the Weimar constitutional experiment and the future did not seem hopeless. But only a few weeks after the book's publication, the stock market crashed on Wall Street, sending tremors all over Europe and especially Germany.

Berlin Alexanderplatz contains a stunning premonition not just of chaos but of something far worse and murderous that succeeds it, and also of the general instability of cities in the 20th and 21st centuries, including those in the developing world. Berlin, in Döblin's rendering, is "Sodom on the eve of its destruction."[2] Döblin's book is hard to read, almost plotless. It is filled with cluttered rhythms and long asides, and its low-down, scummy characters go from one petty disaster to another. But the book is also full of sound and streetwise wisdom. Listen:

"On Alexanderplatz they're tearing up the road for the underground railway. People are made to walk on duckboards. The trams cross the square and head up Alexander- and Munzstrasse to get to Rosenthaler Tor. . . . In the streets, there's one house after another. They are full of people, from cellar to attic. . . . The tenancy protection law isn't worth the paper it's written on. Rents are going up all the time. The middle class are finding themselves out on the street, bailiffs and debt collectors are making hay." The protagonist, Franz Biberkopf, an ex-con, sells far-right-wing newspapers on the street. "Not that he's got anything against the Jews, but he is a supporter of order," says the narrator. The book concludes with a vision of people, arms linked, "marching into war," now that "the old world is doomed."[3]

Doom is the word that immediately comes to mind when thinking about the Weimar Republic. Weimar is a candy-coated horror tale: a cradle of modernity that gave birth to fascism and totalitarianism. Weimar signifies an artistically and intellectually vibrant period—defined by the novels of Thomas Mann and Hermann Hesse, the expressionist poetry of Rainer Maria Rilke, the atonal music of Arnold Schönberg, the design and architectural experimentation of the Bauhaus—a period replete with so much social and cultural experimentation, yet packed with nasty racial and religious tensions, to say nothing of inflation and depression, all leading, without skipping a beat, to . . . Hitler. Yes, we all know how it ends. But its participants, caught in freeze-frame in the act of everything that they were doing, could have no idea what was in store for them.

Will we be any the wiser?

I ask because Weimar now beckons us.

But not at all in the way we think.

We think about Weimar only in terms of the weakening of American democracy. While we should really think about it in terms of the world.

AT THE MOMENT, we rush headlong into a soulless and gleaming future, our lives grimly routinized and yet full of overwhelming possibilities, determined by gadgetry that we cannot do without. Technology has made us both masters and victims to a previously unimaginable degree. We believe we can defy gravity, yet we are weighed down by a mountain of worries that arrive instantly in our devices. This is a very claustrophobic and intimate world, yet also limitless: we may be connected with friends and relations around the globe, but just as often the people in the house or apartment next to ours might as well be in another universe. This alienation carries over from our neighborhoods to our politics. Politics has rarely before been played out on such an intense, globe-spanning, and consequential level, even as electronic communications have made it abstract and therefore more extreme—creating vast political distances between even our closest neighbors.

Yet, technology has also contracted our world, erasing the distance across oceans and between continents. We directly experience the burgeoning of new cities defined by technology and glittering financial centers, which vaguely look the same no matter the hemisphere or latitude where they are located. The future is here, and wherever we are, we are stuck in traffic.

We are building a truly global civilization that connects us all, and that is the challenge. Precisely because this global civilization is still in the act of becoming, and has not yet arrived, and will not arrive for some time, there is this phenomenon of both intimacy and distance between the various parts of the globe. True globalization is still an illusion until technology and world governance advance a few more orders of magnitude. Yet we dramatically affect each other and depend upon each other, so that we all inhabit the same, highly unstable global system. It is like in Sartre's play *No Exit,* in which the three characters are locked in a small room and torment each other. With no mirrors on the walls, they only know themselves by the gaze of the others upon them. Indeed, we are liberated and oppressed by *connectedness,* with the media increasingly directing governments rather than the other way around. Russia and America, China and America, Russia and China, to say nothing of the mid-level and smaller powers, are all, because of their tense standoffs and the way that technology continues to contract the earth, running a strange simulation of the Weimar Republic: that weak and wobbly political organism that governed Germany for fifteen years from the ashes of World War I to the ascension of Adolf Hitler. The entire world is one big Weimar now, connected enough for one part to mortally influence the other parts, yet not connected enough to be politically coherent. Like the various parts of the Weimar Republic, we find ourselves in an exceedingly fragile phase of technological and political transition.

I see no Hitler in our midst, or even a totalitarian world state. But don't assume that the next phase of history will provide any relief to the present one. It is in the spirit of caution that I raise the subject of Weimar.

ANALOGIES CAN BE FUTILE, I know, since no thing is exactly like another. Analogies can lead us down a perilous path. Yet they are often the only way to communicate and explain. While on the one hand an analogy is an imperfect distortion, on the other hand it can create a new awareness, another way to see the world. It is only through an analogy that I can begin to describe the depth of our global crisis. We have to be able to consider that literally anything can happen to us. This is the usefulness of Weimar.

WHAT, EXACTLY, WAS WEIMAR?

The great German historian Golo Mann, son of the Nobel laureate in literature Thomas Mann, called Weimar a sprawling and unwieldy "empire without an emperor."[4] World War I, which lasted four long years, and which ordinary Germans thought originally would be a triumph, ended in defeat, 1.75 million German military deaths, and almost a half-million German civilian deaths. The country was shattered, the royal imperial governing structure had collapsed, and Germany was on the verge of social chaos. It was in that context that leading German politicians and lawyers, meeting in the Thuringian town of Weimar, devised a new constitutional arrangement that sought to avoid the autocratic tendencies of the Kaiser and Bismarck before him. But the new arrangement was just too weak to withstand the pressures of what was to come. There was no night watchman to keep the peace between its constituent parts. The federal states, or *Länder,* legislated through the Reichsrat, or upper house of parliament, retaining all rights not explicitly transferred to the central government. The nation as a whole elected the head of state, or Reich President. The President then appointed the Chancellor, who with his cabinet ran the government at the behest of the Reichstag, the lower house, which was elected by the people. Two-thirds of Germany was still called Prussia, and was governed under different rules than the *Länder.* As for Bavaria, which, like Prussia, was a veritable state within a state, there was constant talk of separation from the Reich. If all this seems like a far more complicated version of the U.S. Constitution with its separation of powers, it was—and made more unwieldy by economic and social anarchy. There was catastrophic inflation during the early Weimar years and catastrophic depression toward the end: a result of a very difficult postwar economy, made worse by reparations demanded by the Treaty of Versailles, and by world economic dislocations. Germany during the Weimar period from 1918 to 1933 was a vast and barely united world unto itself, where the rules of order scarcely applied. It was less a government than a system of belligerent and far-flung competing parts, given the regional differences of a sprawling and, in historical terms, recently united Germany. Again, this is like our world today, with its great cultural and even civilizational differences, yet on another level becoming increasingly united at the same time. Weimar's "normal state was crisis," writes the late Stanford historian of Germany Gordon A. Craig.[5]

In that sense, Weimar was like our planet now: intimately connected, so as to have crises that cut across oceans, whether it be Covid-19, a global recession, great-power conflicts, or unprecedented climate change, things that we can all argue and talk about in the same conversation. To recall Weimar is to emphasize and admit the growing interdependencies of our own world, and to accept responsibility for them. So rather than interrelated German states, so that a crisis in one becomes a crisis in all, all countries are now connected in ways in which a crisis for one can contain a domino effect that becomes almost universal. The Weimar phenomenon, therefore, becomes one of scale.

Roaming the cities and towns of Germany in the early Weimar years were the *Freikorps,* rowdy and ill-disciplined young militiamen unwilling to disband after World War I for fear of suffering the deprivations of civilian life. They would provide the recruiting base for the first Nazi storm troopers. In fact, by the mid-1920s all the major political parties—the Communists, the Social Democrats, and so forth—had their own private little armies. Governments within greater Germany were constantly in the process of collapsing and regrouping with slightly different cabinets. It was one long cabinet crisis where everything always seemed to be at stake. Central authority exhausted itself just trying to preserve order, and in the final Weimar years, all anyone could talk about in Germany was daily politics. It was truly a permanent crisis, with one breathless series of headlines following another. The public and politicians both were caught up in the *moment,* in all of its intensity, unable to concentrate on what might come next because the present was so overwhelming. Everyone was hanging on for dear life, unaware of where they were going.

Golo Mann writes: "Divided and alienated from itself, led by weak or reluctant politicians, the nation was confronted by problems the hopeless confusion of which would have daunted a Bismarck."[6] Again, this is a rough metaphor for our time, in a world beset by multiple crises, when one takes into account not only the West but all the turbulent reaches of Eurasia, sub-Saharan Africa, and Latin America. The former third world may be no more unstable now than it used to be, and in many cases it is more developed, but globalization has rendered it much more deeply entwined with our own destinies.

Outrages were manifold. Famously there was the *Freikorps'* murder in 1922 of the very able Foreign Minister Walther Rathenau, a philosopher, intellectual, and liberal Jewish politician. Rathenau had negotiated the Treaty of Rapallo, which allowed Germany to trade more with Soviet Russia at a time when Germany was under severe economic restrictions imposed by the Treaty of Versailles. Gunmen lobbed grenades and opened fire on him at close range.

The next year, in 1923, came Hitler's failed Beer Hall Putsch, an attempted coup d'état that began at the Bürgerbräu Keller, a beer hall in Munich. The event would have a comic-opera aspect to it if it hadn't been so ugly: demonstrative of all the thuggery, rowdiness, incipient anarchy, and general incompetence of the politics of the era. The Beer Hall Putsch was an example of how law and order could begin to disintegrate even in an advanced country. It started when Bavarian leaders were in a rage to establish a right-wing, nationalist regime in Berlin and met at the Bürgerbräu Keller to plan strategy. Rightist elements in Munich, the capital of Bavaria, had long been obsessed with decadent and cosmopolitan Berlin, so well described by Isherwood and Döblin, and its weak, defeatist, democratic governments. But Hitler and his Nazis, supported by other paramilitary groups, feared those same nationalist politicians as potential rivals. Hitler entered the beer hall, backed by dozens of uniformed street fighters armed with knives and blackjacks, fired his pistol in the air, and while surrounded by bodyguards addressed the crowd and loudly bullied its leaders. Yet this far-right uprising, now led by Hitler, began to collapse when it failed to secure key buildings in the city, and it fell into general disorganization, which featured diversions such as haphazard, armed attacks against Jews and Jewish stores in Munich. But once out of Hitler's sight, the Bavarian nationalists, whom he and his armed goons had bullied, denounced his coup. In a last-ditch effort to rally support, Hitler led 2,000 Nazis in a thunderous and riotous march to a local monument, where Munich police bloodily put down the uprising. Hitler, wounded and almost killed in the melee—a bullet came within a foot of him—was sentenced to five years in prison but was released after eight months in a minimum-security facility, where he was allowed to write *Mein Kampf*.[7]

Thereafter Hitler vowed to work within the democratic system to achieve power—ostensibly, that is—which is exactly what would happen a decade later. Democracy, when weak and unstable, and conducted in a context of tottering institutions, is no guarantee against tyranny. The world is big and varied and at various stages of political development, and the Beer Hall Putsch holds lessons for our time: lessons about how fragile governmental authority is in many parts of the world and, consequently, how little it takes to undermine them, leading to crises that cross borders.

It wasn't all doom and gloom, though. The years of the mid- and late 1920s that were associated with Gustav Stresemann—a liberal realist politician, by all accounts brilliant, who served as both chancellor and foreign minister—constituted a time of economic growth, cultural blossoming, and political compromises and reconciliations. There was a distinct sense for a while that things were getting better and that Germany was finally emerging out of postwar chaos. Stresemann's diplomacy virtually removed the restrictions placed upon German sovereignty by the Versailles peace treaty after Germany's defeat in World War I, except for the question of armaments. There was another bout of optimism, at least momentarily, when the fiscal conservative Heinrich Brüning emerged in early 1930 to lead a fairly nonpartisan cabinet of national emergency. However, Brüning's gifts as a technocrat were not matched by his political instincts: he lacked the ability to compromise and maneuver at a time when he was trying to force tough economic choices and hardships, including wage cuts and a tightening of credit, upon the population and the political parties. "Had Brüning been a Bismarck, he might, despite the daunting . . . circumstances, have been able to pull this off," writes historian Gordon Craig, by presenting his policy demands as a matter of principle associated with his person.[8] Brüning's government struggled on until it collapsed in 1932. This cabinet of technocrats had been eaten away by extremist forces in the streets, Nazis and Communists both. It may have been the last real chance the Weimar Republic had to right itself. History is Shakespearean as well as geopolitical, a matter of contingencies, and if Brüning had not had the personal limitations that he did, the history of the 20th century might have been vastly different.

The more abject the disorder, often the more extreme the tyranny to follow, and that brings us to Weimar's last chapter.

Weimar's house of cards collapsed in 1932 under its next-to-last chancellor, Franz von Papen, a rightist authoritarian and amateur horseman without a political base, a man whom Golo Mann describes as "vain," "irresponsible," and "pitifully superficial." Von Papen's government just couldn't get anything done and didn't last the year. Indeed, at this point there was endless cabinet jockeying but no real governance. Yet even after von Papen left office, he remained a close adviser to President Paul von Hindenburg. When asked why Hindenburg, bowing to the advice of von Papen and a few others, had named Hitler as chancellor on January 30, 1933, von Papen replied, "You are wrong, we have [only] hired him." "We have framed him in," added one of von Papen's friends about Hitler, believing that he could easily be contained in that role. Golo Mann asks what is the meaning of human existence when "such a lightweight" as von Papen could at a key juncture "determine the course of world history."[9] Again, there are large, overwhelming forces of geography, culture, and economics, and there are also contingencies based on pivotal personalities. History blends the two.

Only hours after Hitler had been appointed chancellor, Nazi troopers, Brown Shirts and Black Shirts both, paraded in high boots in their tens of thousands, carrying torches, banging on drums, through the streets of Berlin, singing warlike songs.[10] Before two months had passed, all traces of democracy had been extinguished and the Weimar Republic was but a distant memory. It had left a vacuity so great that literally anything could follow in its wake.

Yes, Weimar had constituted a vacuum eventually filled by Nazi totalitarianism. But our world today must have a different destiny. Like Weimar, it is an interconnected system of states in which no one really rules. But world geography is still a factor. The earth is vast enough so that no individual political force can really dominate it as happened at the end of Weimar, a loose-limbed republic that covered only the geographical center of Europe. So rather than risk the rise of another Hitler, we are forced to wallow in one sort of emergency or another without pause, as crises seep and ricochet across the globe. Weimar is now a permanent condition for us, as we are connected enough by technology to affect each other intimately without having the possibility of true global governance. And that is not the worst outcome—since, had Hitler not arrived, Weimar might ultimately have righted itself. There are quite a few Weimar democracies in the developing world, and quite a few of them may yet succeed. The key is to make constructive use of our fears about Weimar, so as to be wary about the future without giving in to fate.

WINSTON CHURCHILL PUT THE problem of Weimar in broad perspective:

Near the end of World War II, after 50 million deaths, Churchill reflected that "if the allies at the peace table at Versailles had not imagined that the sweeping away of long-established dynasties was a form of progress, and if they had allowed a Hohenzollern, a Wittelsbach, and a Habsburg to return to their thrones, there would have been no Hitler," who had come to power in a complete vacuum of generational order.[11] The Hohenzollerns had ruled Germany, including Prussia. The Wittelsbachs had ruled Munich and Bavaria, and the Habsburgs had ruled Austria-Hungary eastward almost to the Black Sea. Those dynasties were reactionary and lazily corrupt. But their rules, which had lasted for centuries, bore the mark of stability and legitimacy. And because they were inherently legitimate, their cruelties borne of autocratic tendencies could remain within acceptable bounds. They were dictatorial without being totalitarian. That is, they generally protected minorities and allowed a political breathing space for opposing views. But because they were all on the losing side in World War I, and headed political systems that had been in decline even before the war, these monarchical and imperial orders were dashed into oblivion at the 1919 Paris Peace Treaty. The result, in a phrase, was the Beer Hall Putsch and events like it, which originated from an utter vacuum of legitimate political authority, that allowed thugs and bullies to run riot, invading the political space.

Churchill might have made the same argument concerning the Romanovs and the Ottomans. Lying on the eastern and southeastern fringes of Europe, these royal houses and empires were more benighted than those of their imperial cousins in the cultural heart of the continent. But what was to follow them would generally be worse. Indeed, the 20th century in Europe, Russia, and the greater Middle East was determined by the collapse of long-standing dynastic empires in the early decades, and world war, mass murder, state-inflicted famine, and geopolitical upheaval in later decades. The dynasties discarded after World War I in Central Europe represented the old world of imperialism, which had held sway for centuries and millennia, and within which were cosmopolitan societies of different ethnicities and religions that got along tolerably well considering everything, ruled as they were by a common sovereign. Now compare that to what was to come afterward, which were often virulent modern states and unstable, uni-ethnic democracies that often identified with a dominant ethnic or religious group against the others, setting the stage for World War II, followed by the Cold War, and after that, wars in the Middle East and Ukraine involving regimes that had emerged from a vacuum of royal authority.

Churchill saw all of this because he was a man of empire: an Edwardian-era reactionary who had experienced colonial wars in Africa firsthand, and, because of his pride in Britannia, was willing to fight Hitler early on, before many other members of the British establishment had even recognized Nazi Germany as a threat. Churchill's imperialism was inseparable from his anti-Nazism, as inconvenient as that realization may be. Churchill identified Hitler, much as the young Henry Kissinger did by way of an analogy with Napoleon, as a "revolutionary chieftain," threatening world order.[12] In both Churchill's and Kissinger's minds, world order may not be altogether fair or compassionate even, but it does constitute the foremost political legitimacy to be had in the secular realm of human affairs.

In truth, order must come before freedom, because without order there is no freedom for anyone. The Weimar Republic, because it lacked the requisite order, ultimately became a threat to freedom, despite the explosion of the arts that it fostered. Human nature being what it is, order must remain the paramount political virtue. Without it there is no one, as Hobbes says, to adjudicate right from wrong, to separate the guilty from the innocent, so not only is there no freedom but no justice. These are the central realizations of classical conservatives (who prefer stability to illusions of progress) from which all other realizations emanate. Obviously, individual freedom involves a certain amount of messy disorder, especially in a mass democracy like that of the United States. But that is not what I am talking about. I am talking about a secure, stable, and orderly political system where the rules are adhered to. The late Harvard political scientist Samuel Huntington explained that what made America great was less its ideals than its institutions, including the separation of powers between executive, legislative, and judicial branches, and between the federal, state, and local authorities. The 2017–21 presidency of Donald Trump tested those institutions, but they nevertheless held firm. Though Weimar boasted an abundance of artistic and cultural freedom, its fundamental absence of basic political and institutional order made Hitler possible, through the machinations of von Papen and a few others equally in over their heads, and operating in a complete vacuum of restraint. In the early 1920s Hitler had tried to violently overthrow a democratic government but served very little jail time as a consequence. That was the mark of a weak system, riven with backroom deals and compromises, that didn't believe in itself. Weimar's democracy was ultimately no safeguard against Hitler, although Hohenzollern and Wittelsbach monarchs, even constitutional ones with little real power in Berlin and Munich, might well have been up to the task had they remained in place after World War I. That is because the very age-old tradition of those monarchies would have helped stabilize their governing systems. It would have made the politicians more serious, and made them less afraid, since they would have been holding up something estimable and mystical even that had stood the test of time. Again, Churchill was on target with his defense of the royal families of Central Europe, despite the fact that they were implicated in a disastrous world war that had killed millions. Yes, history shows us no easy path forward.

Democracy has worked in the West and a few other places

for several hundred years, whereas the moral example of kings and queens—relying, as the 19th-century British journalist Walter Bagehot implied, on their aesthetic, emotional, and numinous power—has stabilized vast portions of the earth for millennia. Thus, to declare that an age of democracy across the globe is now upon us, with new states having replaced old empires, may not augur as well as we think. Always remember that the existing figurehead monarchies of Great Britain, Spain, and northern Europe, especially Scandinavia, continue to play a vital role in the relatively boring stability of those countries' politics. "The institution of monarchy, shorn of its absolute power," writes the mid-20th-century American theologian Reinhold Niebuhr, possesses virtues that arise from "the continuing will and unity of a nation as distinguished from the momentary will, embodied in specific governments."[13] We take those royal houses for granted only because their presence is assured. Much of the rest of the world is not so lucky. Because the world in general has lost its kings and empires, freedom itself has made the possibilities of upheaval all the more real. That is particularly true in places such as Russia, China, and the Middle East, where monarchical rule with its inherent legitimacy has been replaced by modernizing dictatorships that have to be doubly aggressive and repressive in order to justify their hold on power.

As for the advent of democratic states in other parts of the world, the responsibility for restraint and wise governance is now theirs like never before in their own histories. There is no longer any sovereign to appeal to. The reason why the 20th and early 21st centuries have been so bloody is because the stabilizing force of monarchy in Central Europe, Russia, the Middle East, and other places is, in deep historical terms, suddenly gone. We believe we have morally progressed in our values, with an unprecedented emphasis on such things as human rights and the environment, but this says little about the stability of a global system beset by clashing interests, fed by the aggression of modernizing dictatorships in places like Russia and China. And this global system is tightly wound together as never before, which brings us back to the analogy with Weimar.

THE LAST YEARS AND months of Weimar intimately recall the Russian Revolution of 1917, when Russia descended into utter anarchy following the abdication of the czar, paving the way for the Bolshevik coup eight months later. The opposite of anarchy is hierarchy, from which order derives. And the removal of the czar undermined the only real hierarchy that existed in Russia. In this sense, the Russian Revolution is more than just a corollary to the finale of the Weimar Republic. It is a panoramic amplification of it: a master key to the whole experience and consequences of political disorder. And the most effective way to explore it is through the books of one man, Aleksandr Solzhenitsyn. Thus, he deserves a thorough description.

ALEKSANDR SOLZHENITSYN WAS BORN in 1918, a year after the Russian Revolution. He served in the Red Army as an artillery officer against the Germans in World War II, and because of a letter he wrote toward the end of his military service criticizing Stalin, he then served eight years of forced labor in the gulag in Kazakhstan. Yet perhaps the most important period of his life was spent outside the tiny village of Cavendish, Vermont, where during nineteen years of solitude he wrote several of the massive books comprising the Red Wheel series, a virtual minute-by-minute history of the Russian Revolution. Think of it: having been exiled from the Soviet Union for exposing its vast crimes against humanity in earlier books, and having won the Nobel Prize in Literature for that endeavor, Solzhenitsyn turned his back on the lionization that might have awaited him in certain literary quarters of New York and cultural capitals of Europe, and instead in 1975 settled his family in the backwoods of Vermont, in a cold and desolate landscape whose winters approximate Russia's, and simply wrote. Cavendish is particularly remote, with a general store selling "guns and ammo." It felt a world apart from the ski resorts of the other, more cosmopolitan Vermont associated with Bernie Sanders. Generally avoiding visitors for the next two decades, Solzhenitsyn churned out about a half dozen books, averaging roughly 750 pages each, that together tell the story of the anarchy of the Russian Revolution and its antecedents, and with it a warning for the 21st century. This act of sheer energy, concentration, self-discipline, and renunciation of the conventional worldly pleasures and satisfactions bestowed even by a skeptical literary elite was in the spirit of Russia's own Eastern monasticism. It made Solzhenitsyn, a conservative traditionalist who died in 2008, not merely a great man of literature, but one of the great men of the 20th century.

The Red Wheel series consists of discrete "knots," or "nodes" as Solzhenitsyn later preferred to call them: *August 1914, November 1916,* and thus far, as I write, three fat volumes of *March 1917.* (More volumes are to come as Marian Schwartz's work on the translation continues.) Except for the first volume, *August 1914,* the rest were substantially written in self-imposed exile in Vermont, before Solzhenitsyn's return to Russia following the collapse of the Soviet Union.

Again, it is in the guise of fiction where a writer can more accurately tell the truth. These novels are history told in the spirit of the present tense. Solzhenitsyn seems to leave nothing out, not even the tedium of a deranged marathon of sleepless nights in the palaces of Petrograd and elsewhere, fueled by tea and alcohol. He relives and re-creates how it all happened in Russia in the second decade of the 20th century, and he does not allow this pivot of world events to be bastardized by the clever hindsight of historians and the comfortable value judgments of our own time. For his difficult and unappealing message is meant for the West as well as for his fellow Russians.

Solzhenitsyn demonstrates—rather than merely states—the need for order above all else. Order in pre-revolutionary Russia constituted a medieval totality, represented by the absolutism of the Romanov dynasty. Czar Nicholas II was stupid, indecisive, and self-destructive. He had no judgment. But as much as Nicholas retreated into a reactionary past—even as Russian society was experiencing the painful birth pangs of modernization—there could simply be no Russia without the monarchy. Alas, Nicholas was understandably hated as much as his family was necessary: this is the signal tragedy that Solzhenitsyn captures in these novels.

I will get to the czar later on in more detail. But I want to start with Solzhenitsyn's larger points, and then paint the broader picture of pre-revolutionary Russia in World War I and the subsequent political upheaval there, perhaps the greatest of the 20th century, that reverberates to this day and is central to my overall thesis of Weimar.

IT IS A CONCEIT of the modern world, and particularly of the West, Solzhenitsyn suggests, that history is governed by reason. Reason is like an axe to the living, growing tree of history, with its convoluted branches, each cell and molecule emerging as a matter of sheer contingency, one building upon the next—so that great events arise from innumerable plots and threads. Solzhenitsyn in these books provides a treatise on unreason and the subsequent creation of the modern world in the 20th century, in which the axe of reason, as he puts it, is rare, and when it does fall sometimes produces absolute terror.

The Russian Revolution, like Hitler's rise, turns out to be the most contingent of events, which begins with a complex and bungled war and ends with a shaky Bolshevik coup that sets in motion a death virtually unrivaled in history that would kill tens of millions. And furthermore, none of this might have happened had Russia's resolutely effective and politically moderate prime minister, Pyotr Stolypin, a real force for stability and human agency, not been assassinated in September 1911 at the Kyiv opera house. It was Stolypin's death that would end any hope for decent governance emanating from Nicholas's court.

"When things are too clear, they are no longer interesting," says one of the author's characters. Solzhenitsyn knows that a bundle of passions can decide a seemingly clear-cut and rational action, to say nothing of the most consequential decisions that can be decided by a momentary mood: for example, the assassin's decision to go through with his killing of Stolypin. Hindsight is lazy in this regard, Solzhenitsyn intimates, since it reduces complexity to a counterfeit clarity. He replaces hindsight with a multitude of characters thinking and acting in the moment, so that at the beginning of World War I, "the clock of fate was suspended over the whole of East Prussia, and its six-mile-long pendulum was ticking audibly as it swung from the German to the Russian side and back again."[14] Indeed, the life and death of whole battalions of men, as the author ably demonstrates, can be effected by a misplaced pencil movement on a general's dimly lit field map. Prediction is impossible. It is only through coming to terms with the past and vividly realizing the present that we can have premonitions about the future.

Solzhenitsyn's dissection of the Russian defeat at the Battle of Tannenberg, which occupies much of the action of *August 1914*, should be studied at every military war college. Without that failure, there might well have been no Romanov abdication, no Lenin, and thus no 20th century as we know it. As in both Weimar Germany and our interconnected world today, Russia in those years was so institutionally fragile that any significant event could turn it off course. The ability of the Ukraine War to affect the trajectory of 21st-century geopolitics in ways only now being perceived becomes more palpable when reading Solzhenitsyn's analysis of the Battle of Tannenberg—which covers hundreds of pages and is panoramic, immersive, and masterly, the equivalent in typewriter ink of Pieter Brueghel the Elder's painting *Fight Between Carnival and Lent*. As with any writer of great epics, Solzhenitsyn knows many disparate things: the technicalities of artillery formations and field maneuvers; the mental process by which semi-starving, overextended, and ill-led soldiers become looters; how small changes in terrain affect forced marches; as well as the placement of the stars in the night sky and the names of many Orthodox saints.

In Europe on the eve of World War I, order itself, which had lasted more or less a century since the conclusion of the Napoleonic Wars, was completely accepted. In other words, too few were thinking tragically in order to avoid tragedy. They didn't realize that pessimism can be constructive and help states to avoid catastrophe. They took their good fortune for granted, and assumed it was a permanent condition. War between Russia and Germany begins in a whirlpool of emotion on Solzhenitsyn's pages. Elation was general, especially in Moscow and Petrograd. After all, this was one war you "could not reject." "Historic obligations" to Slavic brothers in Serbia were sacred. "A European war cannot be a prolonged conflict."[15] Of course, the popular naïveté preceding World War I is an old story that is the stuff of many books. But Solzhenitsyn goes on to illuminate in his saga how the same innocence will carry through the entire revolutionary process in Russia, in which words like "war" and "revolution" mean very different things to a people whose frame of reference extended only to the end of the 19th century. Thus they had no conception of how history could wildly swerve in a new technological age. They would not know that the new military conflict would be nothing like the Franco-Prussian War of 1870–71, or that the revolution to come would yield nothing like the French revolution of 1789, which even with its Reign of Terror was altogether benign compared to what was in store for Russia. People sleepwalked backward into the horrors of the 20th century, blindly slashed by its revolving blades. We might pause to learn a lesson from this. Because the past up to this point in time is all we know, we must always exercise a monumental level of caution in order to protect our civilization from tipping over into a heretofore unimagined disorder. Solzhenitsyn doesn't tell us any of this; he illustrates it through dozens of fully realized characters. World War I in Solzhenitsyn's rendering comes to define the horrors of modernism itself with its rejection of the past, as we leave behind traditional societies with their neat and orderly boundaries and enter a borderless world. Here scale itself becomes a generator of crises, exactly as in our world today.

Such a borderless realm is defined by juxtapositions. World War I on the Eastern Front begins with the uneasy specter of the blunt fact of national culture conjuring itself up. Solzhenitsyn concentrates on the most obvious, deterministic aspects of the ground-truth reality that our policy and intellectual elites sometimes want to avoid. To wit, a Russian soldier is amazed at the tidiness of the German landscape the moment he crosses the frontier: the regimentation of the brick houses, the pigsties, and the wellheads. The electric lighting deep in the rural interior and the well-kept roads through the clean, practically shaven forests bespeak an "inhuman cleanliness" and "parade-ground order" shocking to a Russian peasant accustomed to the filthy dreariness of his home and village.[16] From this flow dozens of pages of description of Russian military disorganization and slovenliness, with a chain of command and general officer corps corrupted by a thoroughly rotten czarist system. Russian generals make alcoholic toasts over heavy lunches in the middle of a military campaign. A withdrawal is ordered after gaining ground in a horrific battle, merely to protect a general's reputation in the expectation of further losses. At the highest levels there is almost always the avoidance of risk and the rewarding of mediocrity. By writing so well about the past he is also writing about the present. Solzhenitsyn, the nationalist, would be saddened by the Russian military catastrophe in the early phases of the Ukraine War. But he certainly wouldn't be shocked by it.

Solzhenitsyn's sympathy is rather with the middle-level officers, who "all bore the indelible impress of a similar background: army tradition, long spells of garrison service in a world isolated from the rest of society; a sense of alienation, of being despised by that society and ridiculed by liberal writers."[17] Solzhenitsyn is the ultimate patriot, who, with a deep belief in an Orthodox Christian God, recognizes the primacy of culture and empathizes with the military, even as he must expose every aspect of a decadent and autocratic system that has failed its own people. Solzhenitsyn's uniqueness rests on his deep political conservatism, married to a narrative genius akin to Tolstoy's, and encompassing, like that earlier master, so many universes: from the horrors of the Romanian front in World War I, to the exaltations of falling in love in middle age, to the fantastic dinners in private rooms with masses of smoked salmon and sturgeon, bouillon, sour cream, and rowanberry vodka.

Solzhenitsyn sees an unnecessary war that chain-reacts within a society spread across half the longitudes of the earth. It is a society that for some years already has been crumbling into chaos: with inflation; food shortages; complete bureaucratic dysfunction; a dynasty bordering on sheer "helplessness" and "irresolution"; and a rowdy Duma given to endless, flowery, and directionless speeches in the worst of parliamentary traditions.[18] Here, much more so than even in Weimar Germany, is the very texture of anarchy, with crowds assaulting police with stones and chunks of ice, while the police are in turn afraid of the Cossacks. Criminals are released from prisons. Soldiers desert from the army after nearly beating to death their officers. Mutinies lead to the collapse of the Baltic Fleet. It is as if the entire Russian military organization is being eaten away by "microbes." The army, the "most stable of society's organizations," is "melting and spilling away."[19] Gangs of arsonists set fire to public buildings. Entire staffs disappear from government offices. Youths tear down a statue of the great modernizing prime minister Stolypin. Meanwhile, congeries of parties and factions within parties are left to debate among themselves. Loose, drunken talk postulates that if only the government would change, everything would become better and more humane. There is general jubilation. Bands play in the streets. Strangers embrace at the thought of being liberated from the czar. There is almost a romance about the future, about any fate save for the czarist present.

Of course, nobody at this point in time could foresee the vast Bolshevik death machine about to come next; just as nobody in the heady, artistic, and chaotic days of Weimar could foresee Hitler and the Nazis; and just as nobody alive now can foresee exactly how another unnecessary war, this time Vladimir Putin's in Ukraine, might chain-react with other upheavals to forge a new world of permanent crisis. World War I was an unnecessary war that by virtue of its global scale ultimately had vast consequences: the birth of Nazism and Communism. The Ukraine War, despite its panorama of death and destruction, is not of the same magnitude. Nevertheless, it occurs at a time of greater global integration, so that its effects, in coming years, could also have the most serious of consequences, for better or worse. Crucially, it is the very confining integration of our world through technology that gives every large event within it an added significance, so that there is no time to catch our breath. We are constantly being overwhelmed. Solzhenitsyn's description of Russia in disarray vaguely reflects on what we ourselves are up against in many parts of the earth. Are we any more perceptive now about what awaits our planet than were the Russians of 1917, or all of Europe in 1914, and, for that matter, the Germans of the 1920s and early 1930s?

Order, no matter how complex the social organism, rests upon some kind of chain of command, or multiple chains of command. Hierarchy is everything, especially in Russia, which was a huge and geographically endless organism lacking a real middle class. And it is the melting-away of hierarchy that Solzhenitsyn describes in almost tactile terms. Institutions like the royal family, the imperial bureaucracy, the Duma, and the police gradually cease to function, or even to answer properly to each other in the course of these novels.

In this entire revolutionary process, what pierces most through the intelligent reader's consciousness is the madness of crowds coupled with the romance and irresistibility of extremism, so that a minority ends up moving history. Listen to Solzhenitsyn's timeless words, writing in the present tense during World War I:

"For a long time now it has been dangerous to stand in the way of revolution, and risk-free to assist it. Those who have renounced all traditional Russian values, the revolutionary horde, the locusts from the abyss, vilify and blaspheme and no one dares challenge them. A left-wing newspaper can print the most subversive of articles, a left-wing speaker can deliver the most incendiary of speeches—but just try pointing out the dangers of such utterances and the whole leftist camp will raise a howl of denunciation."[20]

Nobody interferes with the mob, least of all the polished and oh-so-civilized Russian intelligentsia, who see the radical Left as composed of a purer and distilled archetype of their own values, and only awake from their dreams when it is too late. That is another of the pillars of the tragedy, as revealed by Solzhenitsyn. The tyranny of perfect virtue in regard to race and foreign policy that has swarmed over our elite universities in recent years would obviously have terrified Solzhenitsyn.

Solzhenitsyn is a deeply moral man of liberty, as the political philosopher Daniel J. Mahoney has observed. Yet as a man of liberty he realizes, as all conservatives do, that without order, yet once again, there is no freedom for any man. And the greater the disorder, the greater the repression to follow.

Of all the characters in Solzhenitsyn's saga who are not fictional but historical, the most vividly realized is Vladimir Lenin, whom Solzhenitsyn captures in exile in Switzerland in the pages of *November 1916*. Lenin, as a contemporary of his once put it, is a block of granite, someone who has no humanity and is permanently focused on a problem. Lenin's milieu in *November 1916* is an émigré world of Russian revolutionaries in Zurich and Geneva: a world brilliantly depicted by Joseph Conrad in his 1911 novel *Under Western Eyes*. Conrad's characters resemble, as one critic observed, "apes of a sinister jungle," in which Conrad announces that "the spirit of Russia is the spirit of cynicism. . . . For that is the mark of Russian autocracy and of Russian revolt," so that revolutions begin with idealism and end with fanaticism.[21] Solzhenitsyn is not cynical about Russia the way that Conrad, the Pole, is. But his portrayal of Lenin is, nevertheless, quite merciless:

"All that Lenin lacked was breadth. The savage, intolerant narrowness of the born schismatic harnessed his tremendous energies to futilities—fragmenting this group, dissociating himself from that . . . wasting his strength in meaningless struggles, with nothing to show except mounds of scribbled paper. This schismatic narrowness doomed him to sterility in Europe, left him no future except in Russia—but also made him indispensable for any activity there. Indispensable now!"[22]

And that is the point. Once out of Europe and back in Petrograd, Lenin becomes the most focused man in Russia, indeed perhaps the only focused man in Russia, a man whose narrow mind—grinding like the gears of a clock—concentrates on one issue. In this, he is like Hitler in the late 1920s and early 1930s. While everyone is debating politics, Lenin, like Hitler, meticulously plans how to actually seize power, which, as Solzhenitsyn's vast canvas makes clear, is, as they say, lying in the streets waiting to be picked up (as it was in Weimar Berlin). Indeed, in chaotic, disorderly, vulnerable moments, the politicians and the intelligentsia can be paralyzed by the singular and fanatical people who have true focus, relying on faltering institutions to stop or slow them. As an eyewitness journalist in Petrograd at the time, the American John Reed, puts it in *Ten Days That Shook the World,* "the Bolsheviki, in one night, had dissipated" the old regime, "as one blows away smoke."[23] At two in the morning on November 7, 1917, as the Bolshevik takeover began, Lenin said to Trotsky, "From being on the run to supreme power—that's too much. It makes me dizzy."[24] This is human agency, the power of the individual, at its heights, though not the kind that intellectual idealists contemplate.

"There is just one buttress: the spell of the Tsar's name!" someone remarks in *March 1917, Node III, Book 1.* "The people are generally indifferent to the various parties and programs but not to the fact that they have a Tsar."[25] Of all the violence depicted in these books, perhaps the most terrifying is the sight of the czar's full-length portrait hanging in the Duma, shredded by bayonets. Despite all of its monumental faults, the monarchy was the only graspable fact of stability in Russia. However backward, reactionary, and ineffectual the monarchy was, longevity had provided Nicholas II's royal line with legitimacy, allowing him to rule without the sharpened steel of any of the extreme ideologies of the 20th century, with all their frightening *isms.* This is why, as explained by the philosopher Daniel Mahoney, Solzhenitsyn came to see the often forgotten February Revolution that brought the democrat Alexander Kerensky to power as "the true revolution and the enduring disaster," because of the utter illusion it presented of a stable middle ground, since it toppled the monarchical order and led Russia into complete anarchy, from which a Bolshevik coup, the October Revolution, was only subsequent.[26]

The "swinging of history's weight," as Solzhenitsyn puts it, can be determined by the barest of contingencies.[27] Had Nicholas not abdicated for both himself and for his son; had Grand Duke Mikhail Aleksandrovich not been forced to abdicate almost immediately after the crown had passed from Nicholas to him; had the somewhat more capable Grand Duke Nicholas Nikolaevich been able to secure the throne following his military command in the Caucasus; had Stolypin not been assassinated; had Kerensky had better political instincts and been more than just a gifted and inspiring speechmaker; had Czarevitch Alexei's hemophilia not distorted the life and politics of the royal family—much might have been different. The Bolsheviks might not have gained control in the way that they did and when they did. As in Weimar, the wages of disorder meant that too much hung on a thread, and because the Russian Revolution itself hung on a thread, so did the trajectory of the 20th century.

The seminal crime of the 20th century, which given the various regimes to come in Russia, carried over with its second- and third-order effects into the 21st century, was the murder of Nicholas II's family, including all the children, in July 1918 in Ekaterinburg, probably ordered by Lenin himself. If you could deliberately kill children at point-blank range with guns and bayonets, *well then,* you could kill millions.

We can also include the murder of the entire Iraqi royal family in July 1958 by Nasserite military officers, forty years to the month after the killing of the Romanovs, which led to a line of radical military dictators culminating in Saddam Hussein. Then there was the forced abdication of Shah Mohammed Reza Pahlavi in Iran, just as he was contemplating reforms, which led to the Islamic Revolution. If the Pahlavi dynasty had remained on the throne,

Iran might have evolved in the late 20th century into a pro-Western constitutional monarchy and, in economic terms, become a Middle Eastern version of South Korea.

To repeat, it was Churchill who preferred the restoration of the Romanovs and Hohenzollerns both, if only as figureheads, to prevent a Lenin or Hitler. In its first few months alone, Lenin's secret police executed almost 15,000 people, nearly twice the number of those executed by the Romanovs in the entire previous hundred years.[28] This then was the 20th century: the axe-like ending of the old world with all of its stabilizing traditions, allowing for the rise of abstract and utopian movements from the Nazis to the Bolsheviks to Pol Pot and Ayatollah Khomeini, each in its own way constituting a dictatorship of perfect virtue, since in each case ideology was paramount. For, as Kissinger wrote in *A World Restored,* "the most fundamental problem of politics . . . is not the control of wickedness but the limitation of righteousness."[29] It is self-righteousness that lies at the heart of the worst tyrannies: the belief that your opponents can be destroyed because they are in your eyes fundamentally illegitimate. This is what the vast anarchy across the whole of Russia finally wrought. Solzhenitsyn was a conservative because he believed in tradition, and therefore in moderation. His Red Wheel warns of a future with all its terrifying technological and ideological innovations. It can never be out of date.

OF COURSE, THERE WILL be no return in the 21st century to anything approaching monarchy, with its inherent legitimacy that staves off the compulsion for extremist ideology and violent control. We are now completely on our own in a world made intimate by technology, with its tendency to be destabilized by simplistic social-media slogans and fragile financial dominoes; and though its individual parts may in significant measure be moderately and democratically governed, its very close interactions, including the shattering of powers from within, great and small, make for a geopolitical Weimar.

In this geopolitical Weimar, while monarchical rule, aside from the Arabian Peninsula with its kings and sultans and emirs, has faded into near-oblivion, the legacy of totalitarianism, especially Communism, remains both overbearing and deadening, contributing to our underlying instability. China and North Korea are still officially Communist societies, while three-quarters of a century of Communism, including decades of Stalinism, have exacted enough civilizational damage in Russia to have left its imprint on Vladimir Putin's murderous rule. Totalitarianism, which essentially means that no action—or any thought even—by any human being is allowed to exist beyond the purview of the state and without the permission of the state, is an invention of modernism. It bears modernism's disdain for the past and traditions and traditional methods of rule, which include monarchy foremost. One can observe even today the physical damage wrought by Communist totalitarianism in Soviet leader Nikita Khrushchev's "industrialization of architecture," with its "prefabricated buildings, reinforced concrete, and standardized apartments" that continue to deface many a former Soviet-bloc city today and rob it of its humanity and uniqueness.[30] As we will see later in more detail in this book, though Communism died in Europe in 1989, the spiritual and political destruction it caused—never mind the architectural damage—lingers still, and is a supporting actor in our permanent crisis. We are still not done with Communism, even while the future as defined by technology gallops forward. All ages are ages of transition, but never have such monumental transitions been advanced at such an uneven pace as they are now.

Of course, there is more to history than vast impersonal forces such as Communism, technology, geopolitics, and so on. There are also personalities and human agency, with all of their implied contingencies. Vladimir Putin has been the most dangerous Russian leader since Stalin; Xi Jinping is as relentless and ideological as Mao Zedong; Donald Trump, whose political career may lie in the past tense, is more vain and superficial than von Papen even. The point is, there is the raw material in today's world that can force a true cataclysm, or at the least keep this permanent crisis of world order going. There will be no let-up from the headlines, in other words. Forget Hitler. Every tyrant is unique, just as every hero is. And just as technology liberates, technological demons will abound. The key element in all of this will be *closeness*. We will all—Eurasia, Africa, North and South America—be exposed to each other's crises as never before. In this, the mid- and late 21st century will be to the 20th century as the 20th was to the 19th and even the 18th. That is, the pace and quality of connectivity—of *closeness*—will unceasingly accelerate. That will deliver many wonders, of course. But it will be the disease variants, the toxic destabilizing elements, that can threaten to overwhelm us.

Geography is not disappearing. It is only shrinking. Indeed, the smaller the world becomes because of technology, the more that every place in it becomes important. Every place, every river and mountain range, will be strategic. A coup in the Sahelian country of Niger, like what happened there in 2023, will expose the fragility of our world as much as an economic crisis in China. Think of an old wristwatch: so small, but once you start to take the watch apart it suddenly becomes vast and complicated. Such is our globe today and will be in the coming decades.

. . .

LET ME EXPLAIN OUR world by way of the Sicilian Expedition of the early 5th century B.C. It demonstrates exactly how geography will be both instructive and compressed in the mid-21st century. For decades, strategists have used this military adventure of ancient Athens, documented by Thucydides, as a metaphor for both the Vietnam and Iraq wars. Athens had gone to war in support of allies in far-off Sicily, only to become embroiled for a number of years in a military quagmire there. After steeply building up its invasion force, Athens had to retreat with its reputation in tatters. Sicily is next door to Greece, whereas Vietnam and Iraq are half a world removed from the United States. Yet, as we know, the contraction of geography on account of transportation technology has rendered Vietnam and Iraq as close to America in practical terms as Sicily was to Greece; or, put another way, the absence of such technology in 5th century B.C. Athens rendered Sicily as distant as Vietnam and Iraq were to America. Thus, in either case, the analogy holds.

The same might be said for the world situation and Weimar.

Because of digital communications, intercontinental missiles, jet travel, space satellites, and so much else, different parts of the globe now affect each other as intimately as different parts of Germany affected each other in the 1920s and early 1930s. Of course, Germany had one language, and did not have oceans to divide it. So the differences between this world and Weimar are vast, yet the similarities are intriguing. Again, the shrinkage of geography has offered us an analogy, however imperfect, that did not previously exist.

Will this new global Weimar have the cataclysmic fate of the old German one? Or will it find a measure of stability like in 1920s Germany during the years of Gustav Stresemann? For that interregnum might have continued indefinitely were it not for the Great

Depression that afflicted the entire developed world and sent Weimar spiraling downward. Hitler was not inevitable. There were other possibilities. Nevertheless, keep in mind that we increasingly have crises that unify the world while at the same time threatening it, and also dividing it. Covid-19 and climate change have, despite all the trouble they have caused, and will cause, not had the very targeted and cataclysmic effect on the globe as, for example, the Great Depression had on Germany, which brought Hitler to power. But give it all time. Climate change and pandemics are relentless, especially given absolute rises in population for a few decades yet in parts of the world, and by people increasingly living in environmentally fragile zones, subject to landslides, rising sea levels, and the like. And this is to say nothing of wars and great-power fractures.

And thus now we come to our own world.

JOHN VON NEUMANN WAS a brilliant and visionary child prodigy who grew up in the decadent, eclectic culture of late Habsburg Budapest and immigrated to the United States to escape Hitler. Able to quote Voltaire, Goethe, and Thucydides by heart, he also worked on developing both the atomic and hydrogen bombs.[31] Few have ever combined such literary, historical, and scientific genius. To call him one of the great mathematicians of his day, which he undoubtably was, would be to diminish him. In the middle of the 20th century, von Neumann contended that a sparsely populated planetary geography had always acted to constrain both military and technological advances. Guns could fire farther and farther away and be more accurate, but the earth was still a big place and could therefore absorb almost any shock due to empty space and sparsely inhabited territory. Yet von Neumann worried that geography was starting to lose the battle. The earth's finite size would increasingly be a force for instability, as populations expanded and military hardware and computer software ultimately condensed distances on the geopolitical map. "This is an easy change to miss because it is gradual," warned Yale political scientist Paul Bracken in 1999, echoing von Neumann.[32]

Actually, this had all begun to happen in earnest a half-century before von Neumann made his perceptive observation. The British geographer Halford Mackinder at the very beginning of the 20th century electrified much of the intellectual world with his now famous "pivot" theory, which stated that since the Eurasian supercontinent was soon to be connected by railways, the "heartland," or vast center of Eurasia, held the key to world power, as it was equidistant from all the strategic points in any direction. In building to that conclusion, Mackinder fathomed that the great European imperial powers, by expanding their political control into the most distant corners of Africa and Asia, had essentially *mapped out* the entire earth, with no more room left to expand, meaning that their energies could no longer be expended in faraway conquests of jungles and deserts, and so the great powers would increasingly turn on each other. Wars would become worldwide in scale, as every place could be contested. Thus did Mackinder vaguely intuit two world wars and the Cold War decades before they happened. "Every explosion of social forces," he wrote in 1904, "instead of being dissipated in a surrounding circuit of unknown space and barbaric chaos, will [henceforth] be sharply re-echoed from the far side of the globe, and weak elements" in between "will be shattered in consequence."[33] Almost everywhere there will be consequential and connected human habitation, thus every place will become of critical importance. There will be no place to escape to. The great powers will be trapped together on a finite planet, exactly as von

Neumann so simply and elegantly conceptualized in the middle of the 20th century.

World War I may have represented the first time in such stark terms that the great powers of Europe and North America were all bound up in one system. But attrition of the same adds up to big change. Indeed, World War II saw all the major continents of the temperate zone—Europe, North America, and Asia—integrated into the same destructive conflict system: a world system that was only deepened and intensified during the almost-half-century-long Cold War. And since then, into the 2020s, there has been a steady advance of technology that has made the world and its conflicts increasingly claustrophobic. A crisis in one part of the earth can easily and instantaneously migrate to the other side of the earth. Because every place is strategic, the possibilities of conflict become more numerous than ever. And yet no world government has ever been on the horizon. The United Nations has served either as an extension of great-power conflicts, without mitigating them, or as a forum for action on those conflicts, particularly in the far-off corners of the developing world, like sub-Saharan Africa, that the great powers at least deem secondary or nonessential. As for global institutions like the G7 or G20, the more accurate description, as Eurasia Group president Ian Bremmer has noted, is G-Zero. That is, no group of countries can consistently work together in order to alleviate the world's individual crises. The Ukraine War has been a matter between Russia and the United States. NATO unity was not the key factor allowing the Ukrainians to survive as impressively as they did for months on end: they survived because of the gargantuan power of the U.S. economy and defense establishment, which allowed for the transfer of many tens of billions of dollars in arms to Kyiv, next to which aid from Europe was less significant. The fact is that no supranational institution can ultimately replace the self-interest of states: something that is itself founded on the naked needs of the mass of citizens—average people rather than of the enlightened liberal few. Progress on global issues like climate change and world poverty generate more headlines than dramatic action, given the actual scale of those problems. Meanwhile, territorial battles, such as Ukraine, Taiwan, and Gaza, will generate age-old behavior based on naked national interest, and have far more immediate consequences based on blood and treasure, even as their tendency to interact with other battles elsewhere on the planet will multiply.

Global instability will intensify, even as effete and awkward moments like G7 leader photo ops prove ineffectual and beside the point, because of the way that military, economic, financial, and technological integration will continue to magnify future crises beyond imagination.

Columbia University historian and polymath Adam Tooze has constructed a series of crisis pictures—*Krisenbilder,* as he prefers to call them, using the German equivalent—that demonstrate the overwhelming interconnectivity of the world's various crises. During the Ukraine War, Tooze's crisis map was so complex it became nearly illegible. I counted nearly three dozen arrows connecting in different directions about two dozen points of interaction that included the Omicron virus, the Ukraine War, the risk of nuclear escalation, the boycott of Russian gas, rising oil prices along with those of food, refugees in Eastern Europe, the risk of stagflation, the climate crisis, and so on. Tooze provided additional chronological context with the Ukraine War still raging:

"To make matters even more complicated," he begins, "this synchronic presentation obscures the historical genesis of these forces. Stresses in energy and food markets were already very evident in 2021. The war has the impact it has because it has exacerbated existing tensions. Food prices were already rising in 2021. . . . Energy markets were stressed well before the war broke out. Now both stresses are knotted together with the war."[34]

And all this is to say little about financial markets themselves, whose stock and bond exchanges affect the wealth of the global middle and upper classes directly, and the working and poorer classes indirectly. Financial markets intersect with all of Tooze's above crises by registering the level of risk and instability they entail. Now that technology has united financial markets the world over, in addition to wealth-generating mechanisms they are extensions of military and ideological conflict systems, and will become more so in an age of total war, the new hallmark of Russian and Chinese strategy: in which the enemy seeks not only to inflict damage on the conventional battlefield and on key infrastructure, but also to inflict economic pain and demoralize the population through disinformation. This is how geopolitics will become more integrated with market fluctuations.

It is true that two decades of warfare involving the United States in the Middle East did not affect stock markets very much, which relatively easily priced in disruptions in the oil market. On the other hand, the Ukraine War, by intersecting with many of the other crises on Tooze's map, certainly has had a slightly downward effect on markets by contributing to inflation through supply chain disruptions. In fact, the combination of Covid-19 and the Ukraine War, two things one wouldn't ordinarily combine in the same category, by disrupting supply chains contributed to a measure of inflation and deglobalization.[35]

Keep in mind that whatever the effect the Ukraine War has had on other crises—supply chains, food, oil, nuclear threats, financial markets—Ukraine and Russia are still exceedingly small parts of the world economy, thus the war provided but a taste of what may be in store for us. Nevertheless, a war lasting only a few days in the South and East China seas, or in Taiwan, bringing the world's three largest economies—the United States, China, Japan—to blows with high-end weaponry, could affect markets drastically, and obviously for the worse. And that's even if the war does not spread beyond those two maritime spheres, which may be doubtful in this cyber and digital age.

There are also other things to consider.

What if such a war goes on for weeks, if not longer? Artificial intelligence (AI) will play a role in naval weapons systems of the near- and middle-term future, perhaps setting off responses and chain reactions that take missile and other attacks further than any of the warring parties in the Pacific intend: deep into the interior of China, for example, where Chinese missile batteries are located. Forget World War II naval battles like the Battle of the Philippine Sea. This will be a battle of automated weapons and space-based navigational systems. The rivalry between the United States and China, unlike the Cold War rivalry between the United States and the Soviet Union, is layered in arcane features such as debt valuations and high finance as well as in those weapons systems, as both countries' economies are delicately interlinked. China, as the world's second-largest economy, will be even harder to boycott than Russia during the Ukraine War. Such a war between China and the United States could embroil the world economy in a so-called doom loop. And as for the military aspect of such a war, do not expect the Chinese to be as incompetent in their strategy and war machine as the Russians initially were. The Chinese are great students of war. They studied obsessively the American-led intervention in the Balkans in the 1990s, as well as the two Gulf wars. We can therefore assume that they have studied every aspect of the Ukraine War: military, political, and economic. If they ever do decide to invade Taiwan, they will be better equipped to do so precisely because of lessons learned from observing Ukraine. Or on the other hand, the spectacle of vast American military aid to Ukraine might also dissuade China from ever attempting such an invasion.

In any case, the specter of years or decades of strategic competition between the United States and China will not merely constitute another cold war—an antiquated term for an earlier age of technology. While the old Soviet Union did not have an economy as such, China's economy and cutting-edge consumer products and digital networks are deeply integrated into Western markets. (Of course, geopolitics did, in fact, affect world markets to a limited degree during the Cold War, yet this trend is now about to increase by multiples.) The fact that a military conflict in the breadbasket of Ukraine halted grain deliveries to needy Middle Eastern and African countries for a time, driving up worldwide commodity prices, was a relatively simple and mechanical phenomenon, of the kind we have seen in past ages of warfare. But the geopolitical fault line between the United States and China could yet have the most profound and unpredictable consequences on supply chains and digital operating systems. This is because complexity leads to fragility, in which any of innumerable nodal points under attack can disrupt a system as a whole. We may be able to more easily predict the second- and third-order effects of a nuclear weapon being detonated in a war than we can predict the effects of a massive cyber conflict, in which redlines have yet to be clearly delineated. We don't even know the limits of cyber and information warfare, enhanced by artificial intelligence, which conceivably could do far more damage in different ways than a nuclear exchange. The cyberattacks we have thus far seen have been limited in scope, such as hacking a company's computer system or even, as the Chinese have done, hacking into the Pentagon's personnel files. But such things as taking down a leading world stock market or electric power grid may soon be within the capabilities of criminal groups and certain states. Cyberattacks could spread in unintended and unknown ways, like chemical or biological attacks.[36] We are still at a primitive stage of this phenomenon, and at a relatively early stage of diplomacy in regulating it.

Of course, the optimists can also be right. So I do realize how obsessively negative I am being. After all, among so many other good developments, extreme world poverty has decreased, technology is defeating disease, people are living longer and longer. But it is precisely those and many other kinds of technological breakthroughs that will go alongside (as well as intensify) destabilizing interactions among states and groups, and people and markets, even as new and striving middle classes arising out of poverty incessantly demand more and more of their governments. Middle classes are ungrateful. They want more and *more*. This is to say nothing of the building of ever more precise and lethal weapons systems for a species that has not known a century of peace in its hundreds of thousands of years of existence. Thus, I am warning in the tradition of anxious foresight. "Optimism and pessimism can be perilous attitudes that undergird policy. But of the two, optimism is apt to kill with greater certainty," writes Colin S. Gray, the late British American scholar on geopolitics and military affairs. "Whereas pessimism may inspire a grand strategy and especially defense preparation . . . optimism has the potential to risk national safety and even international order more generally."[37]

Thus, I will continue in this vein.

WHILE CYBER WEAPONS AND forms of artificial intelligence may supersede them in destructive power, we also need to remember that nuclear weapons, a mid-20th-century creation, are still with us.

In 1957, a thirty-four-year-old Henry Kissinger in his book *Nuclear Weapons and Foreign Policy* defined the problem we presently face. Though the obvious danger back then was thermonuclear war between the United States and the Soviet Union, Kissinger said the less obvious but more likely threat was a limited war using smaller tactical nuclear weapons mixed with conventional ones. In such a limited war, he explained, "the psychological equation is, paradoxically, constantly shifting *against* the side which seems to be winning," since the closer that side comes to victory, the more likely it is that the weaker side will resort to nuclear weapons. What's more, the introduction of nuclear weapons in such a war would occur "under the worst possible conditions . . . in the confusion of battle," with each side having "no previous experience to serve as a guide."[38] Of course, this was an issue in 2022 and 2023 in the Ukraine War, when the Russians were losing, or at least not achieving their stated goals, and with President Vladimir Putin indirectly threatening the use of low-yield tactical nuclear weapons. There is also the perennial India-Pakistan nuclear standoff, with Pakistan, the weaker party, more likely to resort to such weapons, just as Kissinger predicted. In fact, the destruction of many, if not most, hydrogen bombs in the wake of the Cold War and the development of new and sophisticated kinds of low-yield tactical nuclear bombs only makes Kissinger's concerns more relevant, as if he foresaw the new era of warfare.

Nuclear weapons continue to have their uses, and not just for the losing or weaker side in a conventional war. A leader armed with nuclear weapons, or any kind of weapons of mass destruction for that matter, has protection against a foreign invasion. Libyan dictator Muammar Gaddafi gave up his weapons of mass destruction and the Americans consequently supported his overthrow and killing, as it was clear he had no defense against a popular revolt, and no large-scale unconventional weapons to use or threaten to use. North Korean dictator Kim Jong-un kept his nuclear weapons and consequently the United States has not risked a war with his regime. Many a regime has, wants, and will want nuclear weapons in order to use them exactly the way that the Cold War superpowers did for half a century: to induce fear and, relatedly, as the supreme form of leverage. Putin has gotten significant use out of his nuclear arsenal during the Ukraine War. Merely by mentioning that, by the way, he had such weapons at his disposal, he got U.S. president Joe Biden to be extra careful about the kinds of weapons his administration supplied the Ukrainians, and to seriously look for a way to end the war, for fear of backing Putin into a corner where he might use his nukes. Had Russia had no arsenal of nuclear weapons, the Biden Administration would likely have supplied Ukraine with more kinds of weaponry much earlier than it did. Then there is the case of clerical Iran, which for decades concentrated obsessively on its nuclear program because it knew that even without detonating a nuke, its ability to intimidate its neighbors would increase severalfold. Nuclear arsenals, or their equivalent, will probably always exist since you don't have to detonate a nuclear bomb in order to get value out of it.

In the meantime, the visceral living memory of a nuclear attack in a war wanes with the passing of generations since Hiroshima and Nagasaki, so that the inhibitions against using such weapons continue to decline, especially with the further development of small, battlefield nukes. This is especially true of leaderships and populations in places such as Russia and Pakistan.

Nuclear weapons came into existence partly because of the absence of precision-guided munitions. Because you could rarely hit a distant target with reasonable accuracy, you aimed to do as much destruction as possible in the wider, surrounding area. The bigger the bomb the better, in other words. Indeed, that has been the story of warfare and weapons development throughout human history up until recently. Nuclear weapons were a culmination of a process that had begun with ancient catapults. But suddenly with the advent of precision-guided weapons, in turn derivative of the invention of microchips, state-induced violence becomes, theoretically at least, more tempting and less lethal. (We saw this most famously for the first time in the 1991 Gulf War, in which American missiles fired from offshore in the Persian Gulf targeted specific buildings in Baghdad several hundred miles away.) Remember that in conflicts such as World War II and Vietnam whole areas had to be bombed in order to hit a specific target, such as a bridge or a factory, causing significant collateral damage, especially to civilians. This point still has held true, albeit to a much lesser extent, in the Gaza War, where Israel, with all of its smart bombs, still enforced significant damage on Palestinian civilian areas. As precision-guided munitions now become the preferred weapon of choice in the Western way of war, the chances of initiating violence may actually increase. The best example of this has been the campaign of assassination conducted by several American administrations, Democrat and Republican, against high-ranking Islamic terrorists, in which drones and fighter jets have been employed with precision-guided bombs. Of course, Ukraine was generally not an example of this, with its vast civilian casualties and destruction of infrastructure. That has been because of the general backwardness and intentional brutality of the Russian military, which deliberately has pursued a war of few limits against a large European civilian population, demonstrating that the propensity to kill on an industrial scale unfortunately remains a characteristic of the human species. Look at Hamas's attack on

Israel on October 7, 2023, and especially the Israeli military response. Nevertheless, there will be wars fought in the future, for better and worse, that will provide ever more clinical demonstrations of high-end weaponry.

And these precision-guided weapons will in most cases be missiles of some sort. The earth is on the verge of being completely encircled by overlapping missile ranges. As missiles come to overshadow slow-moving land armies, the earth and its geopolitics experience yet another layer of claustrophobia. Missiles, in turn, are features of automated battle networks, like the Aegis Combat System on U.S. Navy destroyers, with each destroyer packing enough firepower to partially demolish a big city. The lethality in terms of quantity, quality, and speed of the weapons unleashed on each ship, multiplied by the hundreds upon hundreds of surface and sub-surface warships in the American and other first-world navies, has always had the potential to engulf the earth in violent conflict. This has gone largely unnoticed partly because navies, situated offshore in the world's seas and oceans, go largely unseen, unless of course one happens to live near a naval base. Because all these weapons are sub-nuclear, the reticence about using them is reduced. Cool heads are all that has prevented us from destroying our own world.

But don't assume that cool heads must always prevail in every instance, especially as the Chinese navy achieves parity with our own, and even surpasses it. The Cold War with the Soviet Union remained peaceful in the heart of Europe, with mass violence restricted to the third-world periphery, largely because of the fear induced by thermonuclear bombs. But arsenals on that scale barely exist anymore, even as there has been a revolution in weaponry that—unlike hydrogen warheads—is meant to be used. Therefore, we should not automatically assume that the avoidance of head-on, great-power war in the second half of the 20th century must continue deep into the 21st. The Ukraine War, in which Russia has conducted massive aerial bombardments of heavily populated civilian areas, should have alerted us to the fact that literally anything is possible now.

The ultimate danger will always remain in losing our cool heads. Now you may ask: if cool heads have prevailed for many decades until now, why should they stop prevailing? After all, Vladimir Putin's war on Ukraine may well be the exception that proves the rule. The more businesslike, bureaucratic, and technocratic Chinese—compared to the Russians—would never, at the end of the day, unleash such terror on Taiwan, regardless of their aims, and the United States will always be circumspect in launching any military responses. The problem with such comforting assumptions is that they assume moderate and realistic voices will always predominate in government. But that might not always be the case. And the reason has less to do with personalities than with the social and technological forces molding those personalities.

The decades of cool decision-making, especially in the United States, coincided with the print-and-typewriter age: a form of technology that lent itself to objective and detailed explanations of issues, encouraging both the public and its leaders toward moderation. President Dwight Eisenhower, who represented the epitome of cool, analytical wisdom, is impossible to imagine in a digital-video world of roiling passions ignited by social media. Even in his slower era, Eisenhower in the 1950s nearly committed to launching nuclear attacks on China over the fate of Quemoy and Matsu, islands in the Taiwan Strait held by Taiwan and claimed by the mainland. Eisenhower, in the end, would hold back from using nuclear weapons several times: when they might have ended the

Korean War in circumstances more favorable to the United States at the beginning of his presidency, when they might have saved the French garrison at Dien Bien Phu in Vietnam in 1954, and when they might have quelled Soviet threats to Berlin near the end of his presidency. Again and again, his advisers, who clearly were not motivated by containment as it is today understood, urged Eisenhower to use his nuclear arsenal. But Eisenhower always hesitated.[39] President Donald Trump, who, by contrast, represented the epitome of self-centered, emotional impulses, is impossible to imagine outside of a digital-video world. Of course, there are many fundamental differences between Eisenhower and Trump, having nothing to do with technology. Eisenhower, after all, was a general and war hero; Trump avoided the military draft five times. But their differences are also symbolic of the different eras in history and technology in which they operated. The fact is that the communications revolution has changed the way our minds work. The Cold War overlapped with the print-and-typewriter age, which actually may have been as responsible for the avoidance of thermonuclear war as the fear of such bombs themselves. We now inhabit a world of megacities inflamed by social media, which rewards passion rather than cool analysis. And the new generation of leaders will be products of such forces as much as previous leaders were products of more quaint forces of communications. Certainly cool decision-making is still possible, as the Biden Administration generally proved in its overly careful handling of the Ukraine War, and in its dogged attempts to get a ceasefire in Gaza, even as it backed Israel, a longtime American ally. But thinking coolly is just harder now.

Remember that the White House has always wanted to be well regarded by the media. That has not changed. It's just that the media that the White House wants to be well regarded by has changed fundamentally, in the direction of right-wing and left-wing extremes, exacerbated by a noticeable increase in self-righteousness, and politicians have moved with the times.

This fragile, finite earth of ours rests, above all, on moderation, which this new age of technology is fundamentally undermining. This is what at root fuels our permanent crisis. Remember that Weimar had moderate leaders, until one day it didn't. At least we can take solace in the fact that our institutions, as imperfect as they are, are far more robust than Weimar's.

ANYTHING IS POSSIBLE NOW because while technology has evolved, human nature hasn't, even as technology has made large-scale war more likely than during the age of hydrogen bombs. Man has such a propensity for violence that it actually required hydrogen bombs to keep him at least temporarily at bay. (Violence during the Cold War was generally limited to the third world and did not include the far more strategically important region of Europe itself.) Putin's Ukraine War, like Hitler's various military aggressions, like Napoleon's attempt to militarily master Europe, brings up another matter aside from the loss of protection afforded by hydrogen bombs, and which periodically plagues history, and will, we must believe, continue to plague it: that is, the problem of Kissinger's "revolutionary chieftains," the epitome of the dark side of human nature, men who lead revolutionary states.

Such men and states "appear which boldly proclaim that their purpose is to destroy the existing structure [of world order] and to recast it completely," Kissinger explains in *Nuclear Weapons and Foreign Policy*. "The powers that represent the *status quo* . . . are at a profound disadvantage vis-à-vis a revolutionary power. They have everything to gain from believing in its good faith, for the tranquility they seek is unattainable without it. All their instincts will cause them to seek to integrate the revolutionary power into the legitimate framework with which they are familiar and which to them seems 'natural.'" But while the status quo powers by their very nature seek a "static condition" in world affairs, the revolutionary power, also by its very nature, seeks the opposite: the overturning of the established order. That is why one of the marks of a revolutionary power is always to "fill a vacuum." For status quo powers, negotiations and conferences are a means to make progress; for revolutionary power they are a means only to gain time, until the next aggression.[40]

We can see this process transparently and famously at work in the actions of Napoleon and Hitler, and much more recently in those of Putin, who for two decades kept chipping away at Western resolve through the creation of frozen conflicts at various places in the Caucasus, in the Balkans (Transnistria), and in eastern Ukraine, to say nothing of his annexation of Crimea in 2014 and his military intervention in Syria the following year. Wherever Putin identified a vacuum he filled it. His full-bore, World War II–style invasion of Ukraine in February 2022 was the culmination of a process in which the United States, NATO, and especially Germany kept trying to integrate Putin into the established order and over time signally failed to do so. These attempts at integrating a revolutionary chieftain involved a good deal of self-deception on the part of the status quo powers, as it usually does. (Though Turkey's Recep Tayyip Erdogan and Hungary's Viktor Orbán do not rise to the level of revolutionary chieftains, Europe's pleading with them to only be reasonable has achieved no positive result.) For such failures of the established order to deal with revolutionary powers are not aberrations but the very stuff of history, which provides it with both its drama and direction, and which we can, therefore, assume will plague us periodically in the future: a future that will feature more exquisite weaponry and a further binding together of the various geographies of the earth.

Again, it is the shrinkage of geography by technology that may allow crises in the mold of Ukraine and Gaza to spread across time zones and chain-react with crises elsewhere. Ukraine is *now;* Gaza is *now;* Taiwan is an example of the near future. Chinese president Xi Jinping may be more business-like and less roughhewn than Russian president Vladimir Putin. But Xi, by publicly proclaiming his desire to unify Taiwan with mainland China, by force if necessary, is very much a revolutionary chieftain, seeking Chinese primacy in the greater Asia-Pacific. Furthermore, don't assume that a war over Taiwan will stay in Taiwan and the Taiwan Strait, especially since Taiwan borders the other zones of contention between China and the United States, and between China and Japan: the South and East China seas. And that is to say nothing about China's missile batteries located deep inside its mainland, which would become legitimate targets of the United States the moment hostilities begin. We are dealing here with a war zone emphasizing naval, air, and space power of far more sophisticated and high-end military depth than in the World War I– and World War II–like battles of Ukraine. Ukraine has been a hybrid war: bearing attributes of the past and the future. Taiwan would be much more in the *Star Wars* style of the mid-21st century. Indeed, a short, sharp war lasting a few days in the Western Pacific may be the stuff of Pentagon war games, but we should never assume that such wars will remain short and sharp. They could just as easily become protracted and epic in geographical breadth, as other wars have.

Weimar ended with Adolf Hitler. The globe-spanning Weimar of the 21st century will almost certainly not end that way. But if history is any guide, it will be plagued by other, lesser sorts of revolutionary chieftains, probably many, given the state of our world.

HOWEVER, BEFORE WE GO further, I must address a nagging issue for the reader—my assumption that human nature itself will not improve. How do I know this? I don't. But I assume it to be true. To explain why, let me confront the argument made by the most serious and articulate spokesman for the belief that human nature, is, in fact, improving: Harvard cognitive psychologist Steven Pinker, whose 2011 book, *The Better Angels of Our Nature: Why Violence Has Declined,* was an intellectual event.

Pinker's 800-page book makes a stark and unambiguous claim: that humankind throughout the centuries has become progressively less violent, and that this trend will continue. Pinker is not saying that violence has declined in an absolute sense, but in a crucial relative sense. World War II killed 55 million people and was, in absolute terms—in sheer numbers, that is—history's greatest atrocity. But once one adjusts that figure to the *percentage* of world population killed between 1939 and 1945, World War II becomes only the ninth-worst atrocity (after the 8th-century An Lushan Revolt, the 13th-century Mongol conquests, the 7th-through-19th-century slave trade, the 17th-century fall of the Ming dynasty, and others).

The most succinct rebuttal to Pinker's thesis was provided by Yale University historian Timothy Snyder in *Foreign Affairs.*[41] Snyder notes that it simply may not be true that the violent instinct in man has declined. It is only that in relative terms the carrying capacity of the earth to support large populations through fertilizers and antibiotics is winning the race against machine guns. Snyder explains that modernity and education have not pacified man as Pinker claims—for it is impossible to imagine the religious wars in Europe in the 16th and 17th centuries without the advent of the printing press. Snyder's conclusion is that Pinker "loses sight of the modern world in which we actually live." Indeed, modernity itself—the Industrial and post-Industrial ages—has brought us everything from tanks to aircraft carriers to atomic bombs, and every historical actor from Adolf Hitler to Mao Zedong to Osama bin Laden.

Pinker counters that World War II and the Holocaust in Europe were not the product of modernity per se but of the leadership decisions of one individual with a mesmerizing force: Hitler. Pinker also notes the statistical anomaly of two world wars in little more than a generation has been followed by a long peace, suggesting that inter-state war—the greatest of killers—could historically be on the ebb.

The British pacifist Norman Angell published a book similar to Pinker's in 1909, *The Great Illusion,* which declared that war no longer made economic sense and might thus go out of fashion. World War I erupted five years later and Angell was humiliated. Pinker defends Angell, saying that the latter may have the last laugh in coming decades, which could see the end to both militarism and the inevitability of war, through secular education and the feminizing of culture worldwide.

Unfortunately, geopolitics and its attendant realism, which Pinker disparages, will not cooperate. Indeed, it is hard to read Pinker without thinking of the Ukraine and Gaza wars, which erupted a decade after he published his book, and which in absolute and thematic terms undermine his general argument. As for human nature in general, rather than improving as he implies, it may just be channeling its worst impulses in equally deadly, albeit less violent, directions through the Internet and cyberspace, where all manner of perversions from pornography to phishing to criminal hacking to identity theft and much more constitute regular—can we say, normal—occurrences. Humankind is just as perverse as ever, it's just that the technology has evolved.

In the end, ironically enough, Pinker is up against not just human nature, but the fact that, as he correctly states, it is often just a small number of men that can cause violent havoc across a region and the earth. Yes, Pinker is right: no Hitler, no Holocaust. And for that matter: no Osama bin Laden, no 9/11, and, therefore, no Iraq War. But that is the whole point. History is driven not just by geopolitics and other vast impersonal forces but also by the actions of individual men: charismatic men, who will lead others to violence, who reject the rationalism of the Enlightenment and seek to be *pure* and *authentic* in regard to their instincts. And the more routinized and artificial life becomes on account of technology—the more that human nature in Pinker's worldview is pacified and feminized—the more likely that the instincts of certain leaders will rebel against those very tendencies, making them revolutionary chieftains.[42]

The late British American military and strategic analyst Colin S. Gray published *Another Bloody Century: Future Warfare* in 2005, seven years before Pinker's *The Better Angels of Our Nature*. Yet, Gray explains the fact of the Ukraine War, as well as dramatically rising military tensions in the Pacific, to say nothing of the Israel-Gaza war, in a way that Pinker does not. Gray, starting from further back in time, is more visionary. The main theme of his book, published at the height of the Global War on Terrorism in the Middle East, when great-power struggles between America and Russia, as well as between America and China, were on few people's minds, was that great-power rivalries and perhaps even major inter-state wars would form the core of history in the 21st century. How did Gray arrive at this conclusion despite very little evidence for it in the world of 2005? Simple. The past is the only guide to the future, he explains. "The social institution known as war survived the agrarian revolution of 6000 BC, and the industrial and scientific revolutions of the nineteenth and twentieth centuries. It should be a safe prediction to expect warfare to adapt, or be adapted, to whatever changes technology, economies, and social and political mores will lay up for us in the future." In fact, Gray explains how globalization and climate change, by connecting various crises with each other and igniting struggles over scarcer resources, can increase the probabilities of war. Then there is the expansion of military activities into space and cyberspace—happening in the same vein that warfare spread to the oceans following the late-medieval and early-modern Age of Exploration.[43]

"I do not believe in progress in security affairs," Gray declares. "I am impressed, however, by our ability to muddle through." For Gray, thinkers like Pinker, rather than insightful, are merely reflective of their own cultural milieu. "Our debellicized West," Gray explains, "is an island of calm in a sea of troubles. Whether one views that fact as a beacon of hope for the world, or as a perilous source of self-delusion, is a matter for individual choice."[44]

Of course, that sea of calm must be qualified. The reader will come up with any number of examples of the West in disarray, from school shootings to the erosion of behavioral norms to cultural decline in general to the decline in our own democracy, which I will explore later in this book. Gray is obviously being relative, since the world beyond the West is even more tumultuous than the West itself, while the West as a civilizational phenomenon slowly dissolves and merges with the rest of the world. And as that happens, again, as the world contracts, Gray's vision is that deeper into the 21st century we will see both the expansion of war into space and cyberspace, and the commingling of both regular inter-state war and irregular guerrilla-type war. Of course, this is already happening. As the analyst and former U.S. Army officer Ralph Peters wrote two years before 9/11, "Technologies come and go, but the primitive endures."[45]

War is just beginning, in the opinion of the Israeli military historian Martin van Creveld, whose book *The Transformation of War*, published in 1991, is considered a breakthrough classic. Van Creveld explains how it was not predetermined that only states would make war. It was mainly the rise of strong states in early-modern Europe that led to regular armies dominating war. In our world today, beset by absolute rises in population in the developing world where states are tenuous, especially in the bush and hinterland away from capital cities, various armed, non-state groups operate. These are people who feel they *have to fight*. To understand them, van Creveld writes, "the time has come to take leave of strategy, looking into the human soul instead. . . . Just as it makes no sense to ask 'why people eat' or 'what they sleep for,' so fighting in many ways is not a means but an end."[46]

Van Creveld's thesis of 1991 has been reified by the violence and political instability in Africa as local armies rampage in the hinterland. The May/June 2022 issue of *Foreign Affairs* featured a long report, "Rebels Without a Cause: The New Face of African Warfare" by Jason K. Stearns, who has lived and worked in central Africa for many years.

Stearns writes that armed conflicts in Africa are rarely about politics anymore. "Those who take up arms these days are more likely to do so as a means of bargaining over resources." Government officials in Africa often seek "to prolong and even instigate conflicts so long as" they don't threaten regime survival. Violent

African conflicts, he writes, have become "more frequent" and also "more peripheral," that is, less central to politics. In the past decade, "the number of armed groups in the Congo has doubled, to around 120. There are probably over 40 such groups in South Sudan, 20 in Libya, and at least several dozen in Nigeria." Instead of toppling regimes, these groups bargain with them "through violence. . . . Africa has entered an age of grinding low-level conflict and instability." In other words, fighting has become a way of life in significant parts of our world, just as van Creveld prophesied. I say "significant parts of our world" because as the world contracts into a Weimar-like situation, so-called remote parts of Africa in our increasingly interconnected world matter to us much more than they used to. We are all part of the same human family, as we know from disease, migration, and immigration, however uncomfortable some of us may be with that fact.

For example, the American political system, judging by its ideological battles, has no good solution to the crisis of its southern border with Mexico. That crisis, at root, is about the failure of governance in a number of Central American countries, beset by gangs and anarchy, in turn aggravated by a changing climate, rising youth populations, and resource dilemmas. This is the American aspect of the global migration crisis. The carrying capacity of the earth is being challenged in a way it never has before. It is only because the United States is otherwise bordered by oceans and sparsely populated, middle-class Canada to the north, so that only one of our borders is troublesome, that we don't notice this development as much as we should.

ADD TO ALL OF this the profusion of disease and viruses on this more crowded planet far beyond Central America, with its resource scarcities, dramatic weather-related events, and periodic energy shortages caused by complex supply chains and political conflict. Governance itself is becoming more challenging, not less so. Again, this is due to the very crowded, urbanized, and therefore complex planet we increasingly inhabit.

"The beast has only just begun to snarl," writes science journalist Peter Brannen, referring to the earth. "All of recorded human history—at only a few thousand years, a mere eyeblink in geologic time—has played out in perhaps the most stable climate window of the past 650,000 years. We have been shielded from the climate's violence by our short civilizational memory, and our remarkably good fortune," he goes on. "But humanity's ongoing chemistry experiment on our planet could push the climate well beyond those slim historical parameters, into a state it hasn't seen in tens of millions of years, a world for which *Homo sapiens* did not evolve."[47]

Brannen has given us the bottom line in regard to climate change, compressing the fear of helplessness on a planet, on which we are "injecting CO_2 into the air 10 times faster than even during the most extreme periods within the age of mammals," as he explains.[48] We are all in this together, in other words, as our loyalties slowly, imperceptibly shift from national to planetary, making my Weimar analogy, which deals only with political vacuums and disorganization, quaint even, as the issues we face go far beyond politics.

Brannen's point about how we are injecting carbon dioxide into the atmosphere at record levels is indirectly linked to the issue of population, since the more people there are, the more pollution is generated. While the world population is aging and population growth is slowing down in relative terms, something that will become more rapid in a generation or two, we are still adding more human beings to the planet at near record levels. There have never been this many human beings on the planet, and each year for several decades will see even more before the human population is projected to level off and decline. This has enormous implications in terms of environmental sustainability and governance in general, since the more people, the more subjects or citizens or constituents there are to govern, the harder it is to rule territory, making many of the problems I've mentioned thus far in this book that much more difficult. The more people, the less geography for each of them, and therefore the more that geography shrinks, giving us Weimar.

A Weimar world is also a Malthusian world. There is no philosopher as reviled among the educated elite of both the Left and Right than Thomas Robert Malthus, whose essay published in 1798, *On the Principle of Population, as It Affects the Future Improvement of Society,* is considered the epitome of pessimism and determinism. Malthus continues to be ridiculed for claiming that while population increases geometrically, food supplies increase only arithmetically, so that humankind risks eventual shortages and starvation. In fact, during his lifetime, Malthus revised his theory six times while upholding the central thesis, that populations expand to the limits imposed by the means of subsistence. But social theorists may be judged by the questions they stimulate rather than by those they answer. And even more so than Adam Smith in *The Wealth of Nations,* Malthus introduced the whole subject of ecosystems into contemporary political philosophy, thereby immeasurably enriching it. Humankind might be nobler than the apes, but we are still biological. Therefore, our politics, Malthus suggested, are affected both by the natural conditions and by the densities in which we inhabit the earth. If Malthus is wrong, then why is it necessary to prove him wrong again and again, every decade and every century? Perhaps because, at some fundamental level, relating to the degradation of our eaten-away natural environment, there is a gnawing fear that Malthus may just be right.[49] To be sure, even as we attempt to reduce our dependence on hydrocarbons, that will only mean digging up the earth for precious metals like copper, lithium, and cobalt, as "Big Shovel" replaces "Big Oil."[50] Once again, the earth is finite. Whenever we discuss limits to growth and urbanization or saving a plant species or some such, we are following in the footsteps of Malthus.

THE TRAVEL WRITER PAUL THEROUX may not care or have an opinion about Malthus. Yet some of his descriptions of Africa can arguably be labeled Malthusian. The younger Theroux lived for more than six continuous years in Africa and he returned there often. Africa is full of fond personal memories for him. But he has seen the continent change and not always in a good way. In his final travel book on Africa, published in 2013, *The Last Train to Zona Verde,* he serves up one harrowing description after another.

Theroux starts by noting that at the time he writes, 200 million people in sub-Saharan Africa lived in slums, "the highest number of slum dwellers in the world," according to the United Nations. "And 'slum' is a rather misleading word for these futureless places—as I was to see—of stupefying disorder." Referring to South Africa, he goes on: "The majority . . . live in the lower depths, not in picturesque hamlets or thatched huts on verdant hillsides. Three quarters of city-dwelling Africans live in the nastiest slums and squatter camps." Theroux travels north by bus and car from South Africa into Namibia and Angola, "a world of roadblocks and mobs, of terrible roads or no roads at all." The conditions never let up. "Angolans lived among garbage heaps—plastic bottles, soda cans, torn bags, broken chairs, dead dogs, rotting food, indefinable slop. . . . This blight was not 'darkness,' the demeaning African epithet, but a gleaming vacancy. . . . Nothing is sadder than squalor in daylight." Each town as he travels north looks "exactly the same. . . ." He asks himself, "Why go any farther?" Theroux at this point is sad and demoralized, wanting so much to describe more hopeful scenes, yet committed to vividly depicting the truth before his eyes. "My feeling has always been that the truth is prophetic, and if I write accurately about the present, seeing things as they are, aspects of the future will be suggested."[51]

Years before Jason Stearns published his report in *Foreign Affairs,* Theroux, who had just logged some 1,500 miles on land, reports that many of Africa's hinterlands have been controlled by "heavily armed warlords" and the like.[52] Africa, including its far-flung tracts, forms a significant part of our highly connected planet, where "anarchy," as *Financial Times* columnist Janan Ganesh writes, "is more of a likelihood than tyranny."[53] Indeed, while journalists obsess about dictators and strongmen, it is the very lack of governance that could pose the greater risk, and not only in the developing world, but in the West, too.

THIS VERY STEEP INSTITUTIONAL decline, an abyss actually, in significant parts of the world brings me to the February 1994 issue of *The Atlantic,* in which I published a decidedly un-American cover story: un-American in that it was pessimistic and deterministic and, most importantly, declared that the victory of the United States in the recently concluded Cold War would be not so much short-lived as irrelevant, because of various natural, demographic, and cultural forces underway in the world that would overwhelm America's classically liberal vision. It eschewed the debate over ideals that have traditionally been the fare of intellectual journals and newspaper opinion pages. Moreover, because of the unrestrained optimism of the era—*globalization* in the 1990s was being employed as a freshly conceived and positive buzzword—the pessimism of my essay was deeply alienating, if not abhorrent, to many. The title that the editors chose said it all: "The Coming Anarchy: How Scarcity, Crime, Overpopulation, Tribalism, and Disease Are Destroying the Social Fabric of the Planet."

My aim was to expose the illusion of knowledge where little actually existed among elites. At fancy conferences and in the major media of the era, people spoke breezily about how democracy would soon be overtaking the world, without knowing firsthand what the world they were talking about was really like, especially in developing countries beyond the luxury hotels, government ministries, and protected residential enclaves. To counter this trend, I visited the slums of cities in West Africa and Turkey, two radically different parts of the world, comparing the culture of poverty in the two regions, and drawing conclusions. What I said was provocative, or at least deemed to be by complacent champions of globalization.

I claimed that in an increasingly claustrophobic world made smaller by technology and the spread of disease, the most obscure places in Africa could eventually become central to the future of the West; that Africa, rather than be placed on a protective pedestal and treated exclusively on its own terms, should be legitimately compared in vivid developmental detail to other parts of the world of which it formed a vital element. Africa was not marginal in my eyes, in other words. As for Turkey, its very abundance of water resources would make it a vital player in the 21st century, a time when, as I wrote in 1994, resource scarcity would play a major role in politics.

Indeed, I emphasized how political and social interactions, including war, would be increasingly subject to the natural environment, which I labeled "the national-security issue" of the 21st century. Whereas the opinion pages of the time, both liberal and conservative, were obsessed with the clashing ideas shaping the post–Cold War world, I concentrated on how the increasing lack of underground water and the increasing lack of nutrients in overused soils would, in indirect ways, inflame already existent ethnic, religious, and tribal divides. And this factor, merged with an ever-growing number of young males in the most economically and politically fragile societies, would amplify the chances of extremism and violent conflict. Natural forces were at work that would intensify political instability: if not necessarily everywhere, then certainly in the world's least governable parts. The most benighted parts of West Africa were a microcosm, albeit in exaggerated form, of turmoil to come around the globe. Africa certainly had something to teach us.

Critics said that my bleak vision was demoralizing. But I was merely following the dictum of the late Harvard professor Samuel P. Huntington, who said that the job of a scholar or observer is not necessarily to improve the world, but to say bluntly what he or she thought was actually going on in it. When it comes to making predictions, a journalist like myself cannot know the specific, short-term future: whether a country will have a coup or not within the next week. That depends on the Shakespearian dynamics between vital political actors and key intelligence that even the best spy agencies have difficulty uncovering; nor can a journalist or analyst know the situation of a country several decades hence, since so many factors, especially the advance of technology, make such a prediction mere speculation. But what a journalist or analyst can do is make the reader measurably less surprised by what happens in a given place over the middle-term future: five years, ten years, or fifteen years forward, say. And that is not an original idea. Ten-year forecasts or thereabouts are the time frame utilized by many corporations in their planning exercises, as I know from my own work as a geopolitical consultant for Stratfor and Eurasia Group. It is a matter of catching a place during a moment in time.

"The Coming Anarchy" began with a detailed description of Sierra Leone and Côte d'Ivoire (the Ivory Coast) in mid-1993, with references to the general situation in West Africa during this period. This constituted roughly the first part of my lengthy essay, and it essentially painted the bleakest of possibilities for those places, which I basically described as countries that were so weakly governed that they were not really countries at all, but merely places with fictitious, meaningless borders on the map. Sierra Leone was in an extremely fragile political state when I visited there, and Côte d'Ivoire, though imperceptibly deteriorating, was then still seen in the West—according to the cliché—as an African success story. Articles in major world newspapers through the second half of the 1990s painted an optimistic picture for the prospects of these places as fledgling democracies.

But my point in "The Coming Anarchy," and a related *Atlantic* cover story titled "Was Democracy Just a Moment?" in the December 1997 issue, was that elections by themselves didn't matter nearly as much as the building of modern bureaucratic institutions. And West African countries, where populations would continue to grow dramatically in absolute terms for decades, had developed virtually none. That made me pessimistic. In 1999, half a decade after my essay was published, Sierra Leone descended into utter anarchy, with drug-crazed teenagers hacking the limbs off more than a thousand civilians in the capital of Freetown alone and killing an additional several thousand, as armed groups—mobs of young men more than disciplined soldiers—terrorized the city. The number of refugees and displaced persons was well over a million, almost a quarter of the total population. (U.N. peacekeeping troops would be forced to remain in Sierra Leone until 2005.) During the same time frame, a coup rocked Côte d'Ivoire, and the country descended into a period of civil war and chaotic, geographically based political fractures lasting a decade until 2011. War in Liberia continued through 2003, and Nigeria never really arrested its decline as a coherent, centrally governed state. Over the past few years, Sierra Leone and Côte d'Ivoire have gradually gained a modicum of stability, even as political violence, tribalism, and crime continue to rear their heads. In 2013–2016, Sierra Leone, Liberia, and Guinea experienced a major Ebola outbreak. Of course, farther afield in the Middle East, the chaotic meltdowns of Iraq, Syria, Libya, and Yemen following either American-led interventions or the rigors of the Arab Spring democracy movement indicated that beneath the carapaces of tyranny in those places lay complete institutional voids, comparable to what I had found in West Africa. (Whereas what happened in Sierra Leone and Côte d'Ivoire was a consequence of the virtual absence of institutions and authority, the 1994 genocide in Rwanda was unconnected to Hobbesian chaos. With a tightly organized political and security apparatus, which perpetrated a crime with a distinctive modernist and systematized aura, Rwanda represented the evil possible under a strong state.)

Modernism, which implies a world of well-defined states and borders, has been especially cruel to both West Africa and the wider African interior, where ethnic, tribal, and linguistic boundaries "crisscross and overlap, without the neat delineations so much beloved by Western statesmen since the treaties of Westphalia," observes Gérard Prunier, a French scholar and expert on Africa. Here, he says, borders work best as "porous membranes" that are not set in the "cast-iron" lines favored by Western imperialists.[54] "The Coming Anarchy" happened to describe West Africa at a moment when traditional culture was still being shredded by modernism and by modernism's false boundaries, but before new political and societal forms could take hold.

"The Coming Anarchy" also focused on how elites would increasingly come to see the natural environment, especially water shortages and soil erosion—in addition to shifts in the earth's climate itself—as a major foreign policy concern. This was far less obvious in 1994 than it is today. Moreover, I said that future wars would be motivated by communal survival, aggravated in some cases by environmental scarcity. The Middle East's diminishing water table would never be mentioned in reports of armed conflict there, but would operate as a silent and indirect factor nonetheless. As I concluded, an increasingly tightening world, beset by vast technological change, environmental scarcity, climate change, and absolute rises in population in the poorest countries simply cannot be at peace.[55]

I concentrate on Africa here because while it is now 16 percent of the world population, it will rise to 26 percent of the world population by 2050 and will be almost 40 percent of the world population by 2100. At the turn of the 21st century, Europe and Africa had roughly the same population. At the end of this century, there could be seven Africans for every European. While the fate of Europe seems today to lie in the East, in Ukraine, as the century progresses it will increasingly lie in the South, as steady migration from south of the Sahara takes hold. Propelled by rising expectations and climate change, people everywhere will be *on the move,* as it becomes increasingly obvious that we are all members of the same human family.

Indeed, Africa is a microcosm of a world population that is expected to increase from 8 billion to 10.4 billion before the end of the century, despite the obvious "graying" of humanity, as populations especially in the developed world keep getting older. Seventy-five to 90 percent of future urban growth around the world will occur in slums, many in sub-Saharan Africa, according to the United Nations. Think about it for a moment: a human population still growing by almost 20 percent before it levels off, affected by debilitating poverty in badly urbanized settings and intensifying climate change, and on the higher ends of the economic spectrum with border-defying cyberattacks on a scale we have not seen a distinct probability. Humankind on planet Earth will constitute an ever-tightening, *closed* system, divided against itself and armed to the teeth. The comparison with the Weimar Republic, alarming at first, may ultimately prove, once again, quaint.

I WILL RETURN TO the social, historical, and technological forces roiling our planet in the last part of this book. First, I must describe the geopolitical situation that will face us for some years to come, as geopolitics is the principal surface element through which many of these historical forces play out.

II.

THE GREAT POWERS IN DECLINE

Henry Adams was the bookish grandson of John Quincy Adams, the sixth president of the United States, and the great-grandson of John Adams, the second president of the United States. More an introvert than an extrovert, believing himself suited for an earlier, less hurly-burly age than the latter decades of the 19th century and the turn of the 20th century, Henry Adams turned away from the bruising political calling of his forebears and became an historian, best known for his posthumous autobiography, *The Education of Henry Adams*. A man of acute historical insight and descriptive abilities, he believed that the actual journey didn't matter, and that it is only the memory of such journeys—the lessons learned—that constitutes an education. *The Education of Henry Adams* is a work of great literature, written a bit sententiously in the third person, about a man grappling with the onrush of current events and their effects on him. A born elitist, Adams was too learned and skeptical to be a romantic. Yet his pen was lush. He found 19th-century Washington a curiously bleak and half-finished place: "white Greek temples in the abandoned gravel pits of a deserted Syrian city." Among Adams's many sharp intuitions in *The Education,* first printed privately in 1907, was one about the past and future of Europe in regard to Russia, which he had focused on while a private secretary to the U.S. ambassador in London:

"Naturally Russia was a problem ten times as difficult [as Germany]," he writes. "The history of Europe for two hundred years had accomplished little but to state one or two sides of the Russia problem. One's year of Berlin in youth . . . had opened one's eyes to the Russia enigma" and the "fascinated horror" it engendered. Adams goes on in this vein, essentially saying in the years before World War I that Europe's principal dilemma was and always would be Russia: a thing too big, too Byzantine, too Asiatic almost, to fit alongside the more neat and tidy democracies of Europe with their comparatively stronger institutions. Adams writes: "The last and highest triumph of history would be, to his mind, the bringing of Russia into the Atlantic combine."[1]

The Education was published in 1918, the year of Adams's death, but as I said, it was printed privately in 1907, so that those words were written in the very first years of the 20th century. The Long European War, lasting from 1914 to 1989, and including the interval of the Weimar Republic between World Wars I and II, would tragically bear out Adams's words about the centrality of Russia. Adams foresaw not just the immediate future but the century ahead and then some. Now, with the Ukraine War, we have truly returned to the groove of history, with Russia defining it, that Adams identified.

It was a groove established in earnest in August 1914. Remember that the Napoleonic Wars, which culminated in the destruction of the French army as it retreated from Moscow in the winter of 1812, would be followed by almost a century of relative peace in Europe, owing to the treaties forged at the Congress of Vienna by the foreign ministers of Austria, France, and Great Britain, which established the post-Napoleonic security order. It was World War I that, at last, irrevocably shattered this continental arrangement of the great powers that had been fashioned by those three brilliant 19th-century diplomats—Metternich, Talleyrand, and Castlereagh. For the many decades of peace that their realism had bequeathed to Europe had made the populations of the major European states ironically unrealistic about the nature of human affairs in an age of advancing technology, so that Europeans rushed into World War I in a fit of euphoria, thinking it would all be over in a few weeks. That illusion began to be shattered in August 1914, the first month of an industrial war that would last four years and kill some 20 million people. Arguably the greatest and most decisive battle of that month was, as we know, Tannenberg, identified by Aleksandr Solzhenitsyn as a signal military defeat for Russia that led, by a chain of events, to the end of the Romanov dynasty, the birth of the Soviet Union, and almost three-quarters of a century of Communism.

The historian Barbara Tuchman, in her classic work *The Guns of August,* demonstrates how Tannenberg exposed the whole weakness of the czarist system: "The inadequacy of training and materials, the incompetence of generals, the inefficiency of organization were laid bare by the battle." (She might have been writing about the early part of the Ukraine War, such is the continuity in Russian history.) She goes on: "The Russian steam roller in which the Western Allies placed such hopes, which after their debacle on the Western Front was awaited even more anxiously, had fallen apart on the road as if it had been put together with pins."[2] Tannenberg, which pitted Germany against Russia in what is now Polish territory, because it so undermined the czarist regime, would shape the course of events in the 20th century in Europe and the world. As Adams had foretold, Russia was and would remain at the very center of things.

Russia, in the interwar period, continued to shock the West as the wages of the Bolshevik Revolution accumulated, and as Lenin was succeeded by Stalin in 1924. The Holodomor, or Ukrainian Terror-Famine, deliberately inflicted by the Bolshevik authorities in 1932–33, but with origins a few years earlier, killed roughly 4 million people, though estimates vary widely. I'll never forget reading in the mid-1980s the opening words of British poet and historian Robert Conquest's *The Harvest of Sorrow: Soviet Collectivization and the Terror-Famine:*

"Fifty years ago as I write these words, the Ukraine and the Ukrainian Cossack and other areas to its east—a stretch of territory with some forty million inhabitants—was like one vast Belsen. A quarter of the rural population, men, women and children, lay dead or dying, the rest in various stages of debilitation. . . . At the same time (as at Belsen), well-fed squads of police or party officials supervised the victims."[3]

This was Stalin's so-called "revolution from above," in which he crushed two elements inimical to the Soviet regime: the peasantry as a whole and the Ukrainian nation in particular. Stalin's depredations would of course continue and grow to include vast purges of his own Communist party and the leadership of the Soviet military itself. This all put the Soviet Union (the Russian Empire, that is), so central to European destiny even as it was so fragile, in an extremely perilous state when Nazi Germany invaded Russia's heartland in June 1941, penetrating hundreds of miles to the outskirts of Moscow. Roughly 27 million Soviet citizens would die as a result. Yet, the Russians showed an ability to suffer that was beyond belief, and gradually pushed Hitler's forces all the way back to Berlin, grabbing the whole of the territory in Central-Eastern Europe in the process. In this way, the Eastern Front, in terms of blood, suffering, and sheer military decisiveness, constituted the very pivot and proving ground of World War II. As the saying went, the British, by standing alone between the Nazi invasion of Poland in 1939 and Pearl Harbor in 1941, bought the free world "time." The Americans provided the money and industrial might for the war. But it was the Russians, principally, who paid the blood price. The United States and Great Britain could not have won the war on their own. Stalin's policy of "Not a Step Back!" was typical of his brutal determination, and actualized in the 1942–43 Battle of Stalingrad, in which frontline troops had right behind them special security units who would shoot any retreating soldier: 13,500 Soviet troops were executed by their own side during the fateful battle that turned the tide of World War II.[4]

The forty-four-year-long Cold War that followed World War II continued the story of Russia as Europe's principal fact and unsolvable dilemma. The continent was split in two: the western half, under American economic and military influence, was free, prosperous, and democratic; the eastern half, under Soviet military and Communist party influence, was repressed, poor, and despotic. Great Russia now stretched literally from the heart of Central Europe to the Pacific. Russia was more than just an "enigma," as Adams had phrased it, but the power that made practically the whole of Europe an armed camp in the second half of the 20th century. Russia, rather than be absorbed into Adams's "Atlantic combine"—that is, into Western Europe—was doing the absorbing (of Central and Eastern Europe). "The last and highest triumph of history" would have to wait.

Not that the "Soviet bloc," as it became known, made for a

uniform and unhappy whole. The differences within the Warsaw Pact were vast. I have youthful memories as a student and a young journalist travelling from the relative freedom of Poland and Hungary, with their more liberal forms of Communism, to Stalinist Romania, where the regime was like a block of concrete upon the people's chest; and from the dark repression but deeply cultured lands of East Germany and Czechoslovakia to the Anatolian-like bleakness and poverty of rural Bulgaria. Nevertheless, this vast eastern half of the continent, stretching from Central Europe to the Balkans, despite its various national idiosyncrasies and different histories, did constitute a negative unity, owing to Soviet (Great Russian) domination. It was as if color had been bled out of the landscape, rendering it all black-and-white, like the tones of a photo negative. Meanwhile, the western half of the continent was swept upward in a dynamic postwar economic miracle, leading to a golden age of art and cinema in which prosperity and social safety nets were the happy results of the Americans footing the security bill. By contrast, Eastern Europe, that is, the political geography of the Soviet bloc, was fixed in a state of freeze-frame poverty, as if from an earlier age, marked by badly lit streets and grim, blockhouse apartment buildings. Thus was the footprint Russia had established in literally half of Europe, between the end of World War II in 1945 and the fall of the Berlin Wall in 1989.

The Cold War's end marked a sudden and decisive victory for the West. This was the result of deep structural forces and the human agency principally of one man, Soviet leader Mikhail Gorbachev, who came to power in 1985, with American president Ronald Reagan and the Polish-born Pope John Paul II playing supporting roles. Gorbachev, in recognizing the profound economic and bureaucratic infirmities of the Communist system, allowed free debate (*glasnost*) and attempts at dramatic reform (*perestroika*), even as he stopped propping up Communist parties in Eastern Europe. The results were earthshaking. Within the space of merely a few weeks in the final months of 1989, every regime in the Warsaw Pact collapsed. Thereafter, Adams's warning went into remission for the first time since 1914, as the Russian Empire did what it had periodically done throughout its history, but not since before the birth of modernity that came with the Industrial Revolution: it virtually disintegrated in much of its heartland.

Thus, there came an historical interruption in Adams's scenario of Russia's centrality to Europe, as the collapse of the Soviet Union under the strain of Gorbachev's reforms at the end of the Cold War rendered Russia politically and economically enfeebled for well over a decade, from 1989 into the early 2000s. Russia immediately became so preoccupied with its internal problems that it was no longer much of a factor to be considered. Of course, few at the time among Western elites thought of this new state of affairs as an interruption at all, since they considered it the birth of a new order, in which Russia would gradually be transformed into a benign democracy along Western lines.

No historian or analyst captured the failure of the American elite imagination regarding Russia at this moment better than the late New York University professor Stephen F. Cohen, who documented the utterly naïve Clinton Administration policy to remake Russia in America's own image in the immediate aftermath of the Cold War. During the 1990s, economic "shock therapy" was promised as the mechanism that would deliver a new capitalist and democratic system. Cohen explains that the planeloads of heavily credentialed Americans referred to as "advisers"—economists, financiers, academics including political scientists, and so on—who descended on Russia with the Clinton Administration's blessing, were in truth "political missionaries and evangelists." These people embodied the "Washington Consensus" on Russia, which was unfailingly hopeful about the rule of Boris Yeltsin, who succeeded Gorbachev. "Optimism prevails universally among those who are familiar with what is going on in Russia," declared Vice President Al Gore in 1998. But by abruptly inflicting an unadulterated capitalism upon a creaky, barely Western, and crumbling Communist system that had ruled for decades across eleven time zones, these experts perpetrated "the worst American foreign policy disaster since Vietnam . . . with consequences more long-term and perilous," according to Cohen.[5] For as we now know, this misconceived policy, by helping to foster institutional chaos and a precipitous collapse of living standards, opened a void in governance that would eventually be filled by Vladimir Putin's ultimately disastrous rule. Indeed, the Russian currency collapsed. Deregulation of prices led to inflation of more than 200 percent. State companies and other assets were sold off at cut-rate prices to what would become a new class of oligarchs. Consequently, "democracy," writes Steven Lee Myers, a Russia correspondent for *The New York Times,* "had taken root in barren soil."[6]

Geopolitically, Russia's collapse in the 1990s (thanks in part to America's misguided help) led to an unprecedentedly benign environment in the former Eastern Europe, as a number of countries of the former Warsaw Pact joined NATO. Russia didn't like it, but was too weak to do anything about it. Truly, Adams's Russia "problem" and "enigma" seemed to have evaporated for the time being. People continue to debate whether it was wise for NATO to expand eastward, but the dramatic and sudden victory of the West in the Cold War probably made the expansion inevitable. Thus, in the 1990s and 2000s, the West had free rein throughout Europe, as not only NATO but the European Union, too, expanded to the east.

In this climate, NATO's military interventions in 1995 in Bosnia and in 1999 in Kosovo only transpired as they did because of Russian weakness. Had Russia remained powerful in the 1990s, it would have been able to negotiate the terms of Western intervention in the Balkans, where Russian influence, especially among the Slavs of Greater Serbia, has historically been undeniable. It was abject Russian weakness, and the fact that China's great navy would not really emerge for another decade, that allowed Western journalists and intellectuals in the last decade of the 20th century to believe that liberal democracy was in the process of taking over the world, shepherded by an America unchallenged by any real competitor. Military power thus became subsumed by humanitarian concerns, as the moral compromises necessitated by great-power politics had vanished with the end of the Cold War, or so it seemed. Thus, the 1990s were a break from rather than the end of history, so to speak.

All this shaped the international context for the Al Qaeda attacks of September 11, 2001, and the response to them. Because no great-power threat loomed at that moment, it was naturally assumed that Islamic terrorism had now become the principal strategic challenge, in what the George W. Bush Administration went on to call "The Global War on Terrorism." After all, the ultimate security threat had been realized: the United States had been attacked on its own soil in a dramatic fashion with substantial loss of life for the first time since the Japanese attack on Pearl Harbor in 1941, which had led to America's entry into World War II. The subsequent invasions of Afghanistan and Iraq, when looked at from a dispassionate distance, originated not with the urge to remake Middle Eastern countries into democracies but with the demand for absolute security, even beyond what the weakening of Russia in the 1990s had achieved. Democracy-building would come later and was subsidiary to the elemental fear among key policymakers of more attacks emanating from the Middle East. The invasion of Iraq, to say nothing of Afghanistan, simply never would have occurred without 9/11, which further diverted us from great-power politics.

For the fear of more terrorist attacks in those first years of the new century was vivid and all-consuming. The intensity of the present moment—the unreal televised image of the twin towers collapsing—had blotted out any thought of the past or future. This is something that will become more common as communications technology marches on, making us less rather than more aware of the pitfalls and disasters ahead. Technology will increasingly deify the present by making it more vivid and overpowering, thus undermining our sense of history, which is an awareness of the past and future. And that was a factor in the immediate months and years following 9/11, and in the weeks and months following the October 7, 2023, Hamas attack on Israel.

Yet, as it would turn out, after all of the drama, 9/11 proved to be a *head fake:* a far-reaching distraction as Russian president Vladimir Putin methodically rebuilt the Russian state with the help of the military and intelligence services; and as China, especially under the leadership of Xi Jinping, eventually emerged as an aggressive military, economic, and technological power. Obviously, we know all this only in hindsight. At the time, relatively few analysts (Colin Gray was an exception) discerned the grand pattern of the future, and they were not listened to. Alas, by the second decade of the 21st century it had become apparent that the Afghanistan and Iraq wars, far-flung imperial enterprises both, had substantially weakened the United States and given its adversaries a head start in the renewed strategic competition.

Of course, even as I write we may be missing yet another grand pattern of history to which the cinematic vividness of the Ukraine and Gaza wars now blind us: for example, a future combination of great-power conflict, periodic terrorist attacks, and cyber warfare integrated with the use of artificial intelligence, which will add new dimensions and uncertainties to warfare. We still have little idea, given the march of post-Industrial technology, what future great-power warfare could be like, just as in the decades following the Franco-Prussian War of 1870–71 few had any idea what future industrial war would be like. The problem with predicting the future is that it usually descends into linear thinking—the mere extension of current trends. That's why the best futurology may be a description of an aspect of the present that is ignored by the media and beyond the conventional reach of the television cameras.

Indeed, Russia's sweeping, monumental military attack on Ukraine, bringing Adams's theory of European history back with a vengeance, had its roots in such relative obscurity. For years and decades, as we know, Putin intervened in one place after another in the Caucasus and Black Sea region—Abkhazia, South Ossetia, Georgia, Crimea, and so on—while the media was occupied elsewhere, obsessively covering the anarchy in Syria (where Russia was also militarily involved) and the related war against the Islamic State. Then, in 2014, Putin began a proxy war in eastern Ukraine. Yet this and the other conflicts in which Russia was involved in the former Soviet Union energized policy elites only in Washington and New York, who had cried out, to no avail, for stopping Putin in his tracks. Those conflicts left only a weak imprint on people's minds in the West, since with their obscure geography and exotic place-names, such locales appeared to be of relatively minor consequence: *faraway countries of which we know little,* to paraphrase British prime minister Neville Chamberlain's comment about why he conceded the Sudetenland to Hitler at Munich. And, in a manner similar to Hitler's, Putin, having encountered only minor Western responses to those earlier forays, kept pushing into what he conceived of as a vacuum of American and European will. Then, in February 2022, with the Russian bombardment of Ukrainian cities and other civilian areas that would continue for months, with vast tank columns now on the move, thousands killed, and more than 10 million refugees and displaced persons, it was suddenly clear that we were now in a new world—or a very old world, frankly—with the wars in Afghanistan and Iraq consigned in our minds to a distant, even older imperial past and loop of history: like Vietnam.

Ironically, the Biden Administration's shambolic withdrawal from Afghanistan in August 2021 may have encouraged Putin's plan for invading Ukraine, out of the belief that America and the West were impotent. The Afghanistan failure may also have forced the Biden Administration to pull together bureaucratically for the sake of future crises. Without the messy Afghanistan withdrawal, that is, the administration may not have performed as well as it did in the early part of the Ukraine War. History is full of such ironies.

Russia's invasion of Ukraine suddenly made World War II, though eight decades removed, feel much closer in time, as there had been nothing comparable to this in Europe since the Allied destruction of Berlin in 1945. Yes, we were firmly back in the groove of history, as Henry Adams had defined it. Russia was still (and more so than ever) the defining problem for Europe.

By comparison, the wars in the 1990s in the former Yugoslavia, with which an entire generation of elite journalists was obsessed, had involved only small states that were not nuclear powers; and as brutal as the fighting was—and as horrific as the war crimes were—these wars still did not compare with Ukraine in terms of the scope of destruction. Whereas the United States intervened in the Balkans out of ideals and after the serious fighting had ground down to a stalemate, it intervened in Ukraine with masses of cutting-edge weaponry for the most strategic and geopolitical of purposes: to bodily weaken another great power. The Balkans was an elite war; that is, the public was not emotionally captured by it. Ukraine, by contrast, has been a subject that broad swaths of the American public have opinions about, especially when Ukrainian president Volodymyr Zelenskyy visited Washington and addressed Congress in December 2022. Of such magnitude is the Ukraine War that more months of fighting there could affect Europe and Eurasia for years and decades to come. The progress of the war, in which a country of 44 million people has had at times the military advantage over a nuclear power of 143 million, has exposed the Russian Empire as the sick man of Eurasia, just as the Ottoman Empire was for decades the sick man of Europe before it collapsed in World War I.

THE UKRAINE WAR, THOUGH it has exposed Russian military limits (of which I will have more to say), nevertheless also demonstrated that there is and has been no world order or international community, no rules-based system in Europe or anywhere else, the more one reflects upon it. The Gaza War has offered another punctuation of this. Different parts of the world were simply determined by their own balance of power systems that, because they usually held up well, were mistaken for a rules-based order that was in fact nowhere in evidence. As the Catholic University professor Jakub Grygiel put it: "An Earth-spanning security space governed by global rules . . . doesn't exist." Instead there are only "regional equilibria" with their own military dynamics "driven by local historical competitions."[7]

Russia and Ukraine had represented one such regional equilibrium, in which a relatively low level of violence in eastern Ukraine, perpetrated by Russia for a few years, along with the Russian annexation of Crimea in 2014, never really made a significant impact on the Western consciousness. And thus the situation in the mind of many was considered stable. But February 24, 2022, the day that columns of Russian tanks crossed into Ukraine, overturned that notion. It demonstrated not just how mass violence perpetrated by major states was once again possible in Europe, but how the previous decades in Europe, during the Cold War and afterward, constituted not peace but an armed truce. It also provided a warning that other parts of the globe were less stable than we thought. Hamas's ferocious attacks on Israeli civilians, including women and children—and Israel's brute-force response—are signs of how primitive forces are more vivid than the watered-down resolutions regularly emanating from groups like the United Nations and the G20 about this and that, because they demonstrate how our world is still one of pitiless power struggles that make a mockery of elite posturing.

Think of it: the other places where equilibria currently hold but which could crumble or explode. China's stated but as yet unrealized determination to conquer Taiwan, by force if necessary; tense naval standoffs in the South and East China seas; Iran's determination to acquire a nuclear arsenal, coupled with its precision-guided missiles aimed at Saudi and other Arab Gulf oil facilities, to say nothing of its network of proxy forces and terrorist insurgents facing off against a de facto Israeli–Sunni Arab alliance in the Middle East: these are just the broad areas of concern beyond Russia and Europe, where, by the way, the continuation of the Ukraine War threatens to begin unraveling the whole Russian Empire and its shadowlands from the Caucasus to Siberia and the Far East. Farther afield, there are the perennial India-Pakistan nuclear and conventional military standoffs, the real chance of war on the Korean Peninsula, and the rising tensions between Egypt and Ethiopia regarding water allocations after the building of a new dam on the Blue Nile. Then there are all the anarchic conflicts and vast refugee migrations in Central America and sub-Saharan Africa that receive little or no media attention. This is certainly not a world governed by a rules-based order, as polite gatherings of the global elite like to define it, but rather a world of broad, overlapping areas of tension, raw intimidation, and military standoffs. Indeed, there is no night watchman to keep the peace in this brawling, tumultuous world defined by upheaval.

As for the United Nations, it has mainly degenerated into a talk shop more important to the global elite itself than to the world at large. Sadly, the U.N. seems to be disappearing before our eyes. In the early television age, especially in black-and-white, it was a place of high Cold War drama that at least transfixed the American public, so that the U.N. mattered somewhat. Back then the U.N. exposed the world's deep ideological divisions but also its fervent hopes for peace arising from the end of World War II. In the early 1960s there was Cuban leader Fidel Castro in his jungle fatigues, speaking at the podium for hours, and Soviet leader Nikita Khrushchev, shoe in hand, in a rage before the General Assembly, defending the Communist system. Later on, when color was beginning to replace black-and-white, there was the elegance of Israeli foreign minister Abba Eban defending his country's attack on neighboring Arab states in the Six-Day War of 1967. In the mid-1970s, there was the oratory of U.S. ambassador to the United Nations Daniel Patrick Moynihan denouncing the General Assembly's "Zionism Is Racism" resolution. The theatrical quality still exists at the U.N., but it isn't what it used to be, and the institution matters less, as there is just too much going on in the media elsewhere, and the U.N. has always been largely about performance politics. That's why secretary-generals of late are less well-known than in the past. Dag Hammarskjöld, U Thant, Kurt Waldheim, and Kofi Annan, for better or worse, were more in the public eye than Ban Ki-moon and António Guterres. There is just something antiquated about the U.N., maybe because it represents a post–World War II division of power, in which France is a member of the Security Council, but India, a key global pivot state maneuvering among the great powers, is not.

The Ukraine War also has hurt the U.N., since it reflects a world of hard military power—where states do as they please—as opposed to the U.N.'s feckless soft power. The Security Council seems even less relevant with Russia still a member, even as India, again, is not. Throughout the Cold War, remember, the Soviet Union was seen as a legitimate member of the Security Council, having been a World War II ally, in command of a bloc of states, and not directly launching major wars. The Security Council always sort of worked as long as its members were not actually at war with one another. But for the first time since the U.N.'s creation in 1945, two members were on opposite sides of a big, hot war in Europe. The U.N. has always handled issues in the former third world that the major powers deem as secondary while formalizing what the major powers have previously agreed upon. But it did so with the assumption of a rules-based order that hopefully would come into being. Now that seems more unlikely than ever. The United Nations, though it seeks to both preserve and make peace among nations, ironically can only prosper if such a peace is already to some extent in existence; so that a world of great powers on the edge of war leaves the U.N. diminished. The raw violence of the Israel-Gaza conflict, the ethnic cleansing of the Armenians in Nagorno-Karabakh, the gun battles between Albanians and ethnic Serbs in Kosovo, and the trench warfare in Ukraine all manifest a reality far more vivid than the United Nations and groups like the G20 with their watered-down, sanctimonious resolutions represent. As for globalization, the U.N. did once give us a glimpse of a global world, but lately it has been superseded by the very messy reality of globalization itself.

GLOBALIZATION, WHICH IS BASED on trade, the large-scale movement of people by jet transportation, and rapid technological advances in the electronic and digital realms, fits neatly together with a world in permanent crisis. That is because the permanent crisis demands a dense webwork of interactions between crisis zones across the earth, which globalization produces. Ukraine, Gaza, and other major wars have their effects amplified, rather than assuaged, by globalization. A Weimar-type world, in the sense that I mean it, would be impossible without globalization.

Globalization can thus far be divided into two broad phases, which I will label Globalization 1.0 and Globalization 2.0, with the coronavirus functioning as a very rough chapter break between them.

At the end of the Cold War, remember, there was for all intents and purposes no Internet, no email, no smartphones, no well-established global elite with its influential networks and conferences, none of the things we now take for granted as the staples of our interconnected world. All of that came about in the context of a world which, in a security sense, was initially united by a U.S. unipolar hegemon, as America's ideological victory against Soviet Communism led, in the 1990s, to postmodern capitalism and American management practices spreading across the globe, creating gleaming new cities in previously sleepy or at least undervalued places such as Bangalore, Baku, Hanoi, all the capitals of the Arabian Gulf, and so on. Suddenly, world cities looked increasingly similar and similarly prosperous, and people were flying to places they never did before. Silicon Valley, which relies heavily on computer engineers and software writers from places as diverse as India, Israel, and Russia, could not have become the phenomenon that it did except in a post–Cold War world. This explosion of economic and technological creativity gave rise to Globalization 1.0.

Globalization 1.0 was basically a good-news story, so that in its time—the heady 1990s—"globalization" was actually mistaken for a wholesale security arrangement ensuring a Kantian universal peace of sorts, even as minor wars proliferated here and there. Besides the prodigious evolution of technology, Globalization 1.0 was about the spread of democracy and the creation and enlargement of middle classes beyond the West and particularly in formerly Communist Central Europe. It was also about the dismantling of thermonuclear arsenals in the United States and the former Soviet Union, about the eradication of a good deal of the extreme poverty in the former third world, and about the rise of an integrated system of global stock markets, together with a plethora of new global corporations with international and multilingual boards and staffs. Truly, a global elite now seemed to be in charge, claiming to engineer reality from above and throughout the world by virtue of the fancy conferences it held—such as in Davos, Aspen, and Bilderberg. Progress was seen as automatic, linear, and deterministic, and consequently the sense of the tragic was lost. Again, there was an affliction of *presentness,* as if the present in all of its vividness, enhanced and constantly improved upon by technology, could go on forever and just keep getting better. The Cold War, with its deep and entrenched great-power divisions, seemed to have occurred decades ago rather than a few years ago. And because a difficult past had been virtually forgotten by America's sudden and unexpected victory in the Cold War, there was no sense of a difficult future either.

The 1990s ended late, on September 11, 2001. It was stunning how quickly a mood can change. One day all the smart people were saying that geopolitics had been replaced by geo-economics in this new era of perpetual peace, à la the philosopher Immanuel Kant, and exactly as Bill Clinton had believed very early in his presidency. The next day it was all about terrorism and going to war against the *bad guys*. One day George W. Bush was seen as just fine as president. The next day there was the question of, Is he up to the job? After all, as one prominent Republican told me, "had we still been in a situation like the Cold War before the 2000 election, the party elders would have gently told Father Bush that his son had good prospects but needed more experience and seasoning. The younger Bush was picked between the end of the Cold War and 9/11, when nothing serious seemed at stake."

The 9/11 attacks were quickly followed by the American invasion of Afghanistan, and seventeen months later by the Iraq War. The greater Middle East now consumed our strategic and historical thinking. But meanwhile, the Chinese were methodically constructing a gargantuan, high-end military complex, with an emphasis on warships, fighter jets, missiles, and cyber-warfare capabilities. In time, they would be perfecting the art of turning technology to Orwellian purposes, snooping on the online searches of untold millions of their citizens to determine their loyalty to the state, and in the process complicating the techno-optimism that had raged in the West. At this time, while America remained obsessed with the Middle East, Vladimir Putin was also methodically beginning to stabilize Russia through a blend of authoritarianism and organized crime networks, following the chaos of the Yeltsin years with their failed experiment in democracy. This also began a period when social and economic anxieties began to permeate the new globe-spanning middle classes that had been the creation of Globalization 1.0, resulting in the gradual rise of populism and new forms of authoritarianism in a number of countries in the West and the former third world. Whether it was the strengthening of a nasty right-wing movement in France or Hungary, or Brazil or Turkey, or wherever, encouragement always seemed to flow from Putin's newly risen Russia. Evidently, the contraction of the world system had helped allow not only for the spread of good trends, but for bad ones as well. Globalization 2.0 was upon us, and it wasn't altogether a good-news story.

Covid-19, which to a significant extent shut down the world economy, struck at the end of 2019, and its effects lingered for a number of years. As the world emerged from Covid-19, globalization—which had dramatically helped spread the virus—did not look so benign. Average readers like chapter breaks, and Covid-19 was a convenient if very imperfect chapter break between Globalization 1.0 and Globalization 2.0. We were now in a new world, and globalization seemed a distinctly value-neutral historical development, as good as it was bad, and in fact central to the permanent, Weimar-like crisis I have been describing.

A world united was also a world where there was no place to hide. The belief that a smaller world would necessarily be a better world was fundamentally flawed, since it assumed an inherent goodness in the fact of proximity, which is often not the case. After all, we periodically don't get along with our next-door neighbors. Countries have military clashes along their borders. Disease does not respect borders. Because of these and many other examples, we often yearn for separation and quietude. One of the reasons America is powerful is that it is protected by oceans. And one of the reasons why Americans have become less secure is because oceans offer them less protection than they used to. Once again, the finite earth is gradually losing the race against technology and population growth, as John von Neumann indicated. Covid-19 spread as far and as rapidly as it did because of this phenomenon. Covid-19 might actually have been a minor factor in Putin's decision to invade Ukraine, since it increased his isolation from other people, which left him more often alone with his own thoughts. Both the virus and the Ukraine War, by the way, each in its own fashion, disrupted supply chains, contributing to an element of deglobalization, however short-lived it was. It is just that because everything intersects with everything else in a smaller world, such a world is by definition unstable.

Journalists began to record an unending series of cataclysms: Covid-19 and massive lockdowns, the murder by Minneapolis police of the African American George Floyd and ensuing urban riots and protests, the January 6, 2021, Capitol insurrection as the capstone of the nonstop crises of the Trump presidency, the Russian invasion of Ukraine and the partial rearming of Europe, the Chinese crackdown on Hong Kong coupled with Beijing's intensifying military threat to Taiwan, the Gaza War following the Hamas attack on Israel, and so forth all added to the crises on the international scene. History had marched on, with domestic events interwoven with world events, and no time to catch one's breath. And it was real history, for each of those events' effect on society and geopolitics was profound. The George Floyd murder changed our ideas about race and the American past. It even changed our language and how we were supposed to express ourselves. The Trump presidency from 2017 to 2021 made us question the very viability of American democracy and political order. The Ukraine War made us fear the very thing we had thought we had left behind many decades before: a conventional military conflict between the great powers. Humanity's new sense of claustrophobia, wrought by the closing of distance, which was in turn wrought by technology, was in and of itself intensifying the magnitude of each crisis as it was perceived. The *hot* medium of digital-video communications drove us into emotional, philosophical, and ideological silos much more than did the cool, gray medium of print-and-typewriter journalism. Journalists shoved their opinions in our faces in a way that was harder to do with the old technology. They were participants, taking sides in a way they never used to do, which only served to further intensify everything we thought and heard. We all felt we were down in the arena as well as watching from the stands. Personal life has its escalating anxieties, to be sure, but public life had become unbearable.

It used to be in years and decades past that the most combative political arguments were about the Middle East, which quickly descended into an us-versus-them mentality: you were either for the Jews or for the Arabs. Now the whole world and much of public life has become as confrontational as the Middle East. *That* is the totemic reality of globalization.

Enmeshed in the tumult of globalization, with all of its mayhem, are the great powers, on which a semblance of world order depends, all of which are experiencing grave difficulties. Whatever the state of upheaval in America, the fact is that Russia and China are experiencing something deeper and more fundamental. Let me start, though, with America and Russia.

IN THE FIRST QUARTER of the 21st century, two of the three great powers, the United States and Russia, initiated truly unnecessary and disastrous wars of choice: the United States in Iraq and Russia in Ukraine. We might also add the American war in Afghanistan, which started out well in the fall of 2001 with tactical ingenuity and an economy of military force, but which quickly transformed into a two-decade-long occupation by a big, creaky U.S. Army bureaucracy—something completely unsuited for a sprawling, mountainous, and underdeveloped country. The point is, national power itself, which is derivative of geographical position, natural resources, and economic strength, is ultimately dependent on the good judgment of leaders: not all of the time, but most of the time, and especially when key decisions are required that can constitute historical hinges. The wars in Iraq and Ukraine show the dearth of wise and cautious leadership not just in the United States after the end of the Cold War, but in Russia as well, as Soviet leaders from Leonid Brezhnev to Mikhail Gorbachev were on the whole far wiser and more cautious than Putin. Indeed, leadership is vital to a great power or empire. It constitutes the Shakespearean element that ultimately eclipses the vast impersonal forces of geopolitical and economic fate. That is why China's leader Xi Jinping's obsession with absorbing or even conquering Taiwan might indicate that not only the United States and Russia, but China, too, face over the long term what I call Shakespearean decline. I refer to the inner demons that drive all powerful leaders to a certain degree of madness, best exemplified in some of the plays of Shakespeare. It is uncanny, as if all three great powers have produced leaders with a death wish, each driven by private torments. And the more concentrated and unchallenged their individual power, the greater their proclivity to do real damage to the worldwide geopolitical equilibrium.

Of course, the mistakes of American and Russian leaders have not been of the same magnitude (even as in China's case we can't be sure, as a military conflict over Taiwan may still lie in the future).

For example, the Iraq War begun by President George W. Bush was never as central to America's declining reputation for power in the first two decades of the 21st century as the Ukraine War was to Russia's declining reputation for judgment and safeguarding its far-flung empire in the century's third decade. Iraq, however much it dominated news coverage in the early and mid-2000s, and however vast the civilian and military carnage—more than 7,000 American troops and civilian contractors dead and 35,000 seriously wounded, in addition to hundreds of thousands of Iraqi civilians killed—was at the end of the day a far-flung imperial adventure gone awry, from which the United States managed to recover, as callous as that sounds.[8] Iraq certainly contributed to the malaise among Republicans and the nation at large that culminated in the election of Donald Trump as president in 2016. The soldiers and Marines from blue-collar families who fought in Iraq and Afghanistan—who I can attest as an embedded war reporter were originally enthusiastic about the prospects of victory—in significant measure turned to Trump following the abject failure of both wars, something which became undeniably apparent around the beginning of the century's second decade. Yet the failure of the Iraq War was never truly central to Trump's election: not nearly as central as was the outsourcing of well-paying manufacturing jobs to China and other developing countries, the further job-killing effects of automation, the anemic growth of the American economy in the years before Trump's victory, or general cultural issues that occupied the media and obviously played a significant role. Through it all, Iraq was just not as important to America's geopolitical identity as Ukraine has been to Russia's.

But Iraq mattered in another, more subtle way. It was the most clear-cut example of the general deterioration in the quality of American leadership since the end of the Cold War. Even considering the Biden Administration's middling-competent handling of the Ukraine War thus far, the record of presidential leadership in foreign policy from Harry Truman to George H. W. Bush (and including Dwight Eisenhower, Richard Nixon, and Ronald Reagan) was of a much higher caliber than from Bill Clinton to the current occupant of the White House (and including George W. Bush and Donald Trump). The difference between Cold War presidential leadership and post–Cold War presidential leadership might have been even greater had John F. Kennedy not been assassinated in November 1963. Kennedy, a wealthy, confident, genuine World War II hero who was extremely well read in foreign affairs, would likely not have swallowed wholesale the advice of the Pentagon to greatly expand the Vietnam War, exactly as President Lyndon Johnson, a foreign policy neophyte, did, in fact, do in 1965.

Such a palpable decline from one group to another, despite individual variations, was related to a decay in the culture of public life, especially the media, in which the forces acting upon all of these men had become more divisive, intolerant, and even hysterical at times. And as the media has become less serious, so have our leaders. The media, with its right- and left-wing extremes, each seeking to proclaim its virtue in its own way, has often encouraged our post–Cold War presidents to be moralistic rather than moral. Passion, often the enemy of analysis, is precisely what is encouraged by social media, which has had such an insidious effect on our politics. To some extent, nations, especially in democracies, get the leaders they deserve. America was a great and well-functioning mass democracy in the print-and-typewriter age. It is unclear whether it can continue as such in a digital-video age aggravated by social media, which promises to be further manipulated by artificial intelligence.

I will go into American society in far more detail in the third and last part of this book. For now, suffice it to say that America's weakness and its capacity to decline is rather subtle; that is, unrelated to fundamental structural forces: geography, for instance. It may be in decline, but it remains a powerful behemoth. After all, America is bordered on two sides by great oceans and a thin band of middle-class civilization in Canada to its north. Its only problematic border is with Mexico to its south.

Furthermore, America has been united by the Mississippi, Missouri, and Ohio river systems, which allows goods to travel from one end of the continent to the other, in turn allowing for a vast internal market to develop. Meanwhile, China has a long border with an historical enemy to the north, Russia, and to the south with historical enemies India and Vietnam; in the east China faces a veritable maritime wall of hostile, pro-American states. As for Russia, its northern coastline is ice-blocked much of the year, and it sprawls across half the longitudes of the earth without properly placed river systems such as America's to internally connect it, and without natural borders such as seas and mountains to protect it from invasion—and *that* is at the root of Russian insecurity that has driven it to be overly aggressive. America is not only geographically blessed, but technologically superior to China even, because of its free society and consequent tradition of inquiry and risk-taking.

It is America's political, social, and cultural divisions that have taken their toll on the country's political leadership, and that's even if Donald Trump passes from the scene. In sum, American society is clearly engaged in a continuing partisan war of sorts, though one mainly without the shooting. Indeed, the United States has come a long way—in terms of becoming more divided—since, as a six-year-old boy in 1958, I watched a liberal crowd on Eastern Parkway in Brooklyn cheering wizened veterans of the imperialist Spanish-

American War of 1898, one of my most vivid early-childhood memories. A few years later the Vietnam War would tear asunder American society's unity and cause a large segment of the public to lose its trust in government, a trust that had been nurtured by the successes of the New Deal, World War II, and the space program. But as I said, I will deal with America's social and political pathologies later.

THE DECLINE OF RUSSIA is on a different scale entirely. For two decades, as Vladimir Putin restored Russia to great-power status following the debacle of the end of the Cold War and the disintegration of the Soviet Union, he became increasingly dangerous, autocratic, and, in fact, outright vicious, demonstrated by, among other things, the grisly poisoning of several Russian dissidents. Putin initiated frozen wars; that is, permanent military conflicts and standoffs throughout Ukraine and the Caucasus. He murdered and otherwise destroyed adversaries in Russian society, of which the poisonings were but examples. And he rebuilt Russia's military and security complex, with a nasty tendency to initiate cyberattacks in the West. But all of this was on a rather small scale. Meanwhile, he had relatively cheap, high-quality natural gas to sell to NATO countries, particularly Germany.

Germany was central to Putin's strategy. Germany, which boasted the most powerful economy and manufacturing base in Europe, had, as we know, a long and sorry history with Russia. Its panoramic Eastern Front with Russia was exceedingly bloody in World War I. And in World War II, the Eastern Front constituted far and away the bloodiest contest in the entire European theater. To repeat, roughly 27 million Soviets died during World War II fighting Nazi Germany. The Battle of Stalingrad alone, which turned the tide of the war against Hitler, accounted for roughly 2 million German and Soviet casualties. As the British historian Antony Beevor recounts, the vast fields of the dead and dying at Stalingrad, afflicted by starvation, frostbite, lice, forced marches, and executions, might even be compared to the sufferings at Nazi concentration camps. Then came the Cold War, when sheer Russian military power split Germany in half. East Germany was by and large an artificial Communist state occupied by the Soviet army. With this traumatic history, Germans in the early 21st century desperately wanted a normal relationship with Russia. In fact, *Ostpolitik,* the West German policy of normalizing relations with Communist East Germany and the rest of the East Bloc in the late 1960s and the 1970s had an elemental theme of reaching out to the Soviet Union (the Russian Communist Empire) in order to assuage this difficult history. Simply put, no German wanted another war in the East. Russian natural gas, transported by pipelines to Germany and the rest of Central-Eastern Europe from Siberian fields, seemed to offer a convenient and profitable solution to this historical dilemma.

Russian gas, it was believed, would solve Germany's energy needs while also forging a stable, even friendly, relationship between Germany and Russia. Gas deals with Russia made the German political establishment feel good about itself, since the deals would prevent another war in Europe, even as they helped make Germany and key members of its establishment extraordinarily wealthy. This is why the German establishment supported former chancellor Gerhard Schröder's acceptance of lucrative and high executive positions in Russian energy companies, such as Nord Stream AG, Rosneft, and Gazprom. Think of it: a former German chancellor, the equivalent of a former U.S. president, taking top positions in the energy firms of a dictatorship and rival great power. Schröder could only have done this with the approval of the chancellor at the time, Angela Merkel. Merkel, from Germany's main right-of-center party, the Christian Democratic Union, and Schröder, from the main left-of-center party, the Social Democrats, effectively forged a political alliance based on Russian gas that took Germany in a neutralist strategic direction located between NATO and Russia, even as Germany was a member of NATO with the United States effectively paying for its defense. It was a good deal if you could get it. And Germany did.

There was only one issue: Vladimir Putin himself. The whole German strategy that Merkel and her predecessor Schröder had bought into was based on an assessment of Putin being rational and dependable at the end of the day—that is to say, despite his being aggressive, nasty, and troublesome, they assumed he would not blow up Europe. His annexation of Crimea and launching of an unconventional small war in eastern Ukraine in 2014, coupled with the poisoning of his principal enemies, was worrying, surely. But as long as he did not do something like launch a major land war you could do business with him, or so the German political and economic establishment essentially thought. It would turn out that this calculated risk and assessment of one man was dead wrong.

While all this was going on—while Putin entrapped Germany as well as other countries in Europe with Russian natural gas—he also divided them by encouraging European populist leaders such as Hungary's Viktor Orbán and France's Marine Le Pen, leaders who, like Putin himself, believed in the reality of the ethnic nation above that of the individual. Given all this, Putin believed that a quick and successful invasion of Ukraine would forge a permanent alliance with a weakened and insecure Germany, practically dislodging it from the West, which would have the indirect effect of further undermining Europe's other liberal democracies. Splitting

Europe was clearly in Putin's interest, as he defined it. It was only a matter of a successful or even just a partially successful invasion of Ukraine that could be over in a matter of weeks with relatively little bloodshed.

Putin's decision to invade Ukraine was not as mad as it seems. In the years and decade or two prior to his invasion he had successfully intervened in Syria, South Ossetia, and so on, where he learned a different lesson than what George W. Bush had learned in Iraq. What Putin thought he learned was that wars could actually be fought cheaply and successfully. Indeed, in those wars, as well as in Russia's mercenary operations in sub-Saharan Africa, relatively small and professionalized units had been involved, given to discipline, proper training, and reasonably high morale. As for Syria, Russia intervened mostly in the air. Thus it must have seemed to Putin that he had successfully modernized Russia's military following the collapse of the Soviet Union the generation before.

But just as the German political and economic establishment misread Putin, Putin misread Ukraine. History, among other things, is a record of such miscalculations. Most famously, perhaps, European leaders in the early and mid-1930s misread Hitler, and Hitler, following a streak of successful military aggressions, misread the difficulty of conquering the Soviet Union. In a similar vein, Ukraine overturned the notion of Putin's own successful streak of military interventions. This is not to draw a comparison between Hitler and Putin, who are vastly different men, only to suggest that history in a very broad sense can follow similar patterns.

Ukraine overturned Putin's notion of his own invincibility. Because he now attempted a war of scale in a large country, not only were special forces and mercenaries involved, but mainly large numbers of conventional troops and tank units. Suddenly, for the first time in the record of Putin's military adventures, combined arms, that is, coordination between air, land, and sea forces, as well as a realistic strategy befitting a World War II–size campaign, were all required. And that, in turn, meant *logistics, logistics, logistics:* coordinating the supply of fuel, food, spare parts, maintenance units, ammunition, and what have you for a large, advancing army separated into a half dozen principal paths of advance. As it turned out, none of those elements was in evidence in the initial Russian aggression against Ukraine.

Several years of embedding with U.S. ground forces during the Global War on Terrorism had taught me that a first-world army is built around its NCO corps: the various types of sergeants, corporals, and other noncommissioned officers who impose pride and discipline on the thousands of troops. Officers devise policy and plans, NCOs carry them out. Military culture depends far more on NCOs than on officers. The Russian military that Putin sent into Ukraine barely had an NCO corps. With the special-forces units who had fought Russia's small wars, that hadn't mattered much. The Wagner Group in the Middle East and Africa and the "little green men" in eastern Ukraine were mercenaries by another name. But with the large conventional force that Russia sent into Ukraine, the absence of a strong and competent NCO corps was everything. This was why a relatively large number of Russian generals were killed early in the war: after all, rather than remain in the rear directing large-scale movements as in a Western army, they were forward and consequently vulnerable because there were not enough empowered lower-level officers and NCOs to carry out their orders. A first-world army, the product of Western democracy, decentralizes decision-making down through the ranks; a third-world army, especially if it is a product of a Communist Soviet legacy, does not. Russia's did not.

Moreover, the old Russian demons from decades and centuries

past of land warfare now reasserted themselves. The Russians were less an army than a mob on the move. This had always been the case. For example, Nancy Mitford, in her biography of Frederick the Great, writes that whereas it was reckoned that in one campaign in 1759, the Prussian military burnt some 1,000 civilian houses, the Russians burnt about 15,000.[9] There was, too, to cite another odd but telling example from a history of depredations, Stalin's treatment of the ethnic German civilians outside Germany at the end of World War II. The Soviets deported and conscripted hundreds of thousands of these people for forced labor, considering this awful deed fair reparations for Germany's invasion of the Soviet Union. A leadership that could perpetrate show trials of imagined political enemies and enlarge a czarist penal system into an archipelago of forced labor camps known as the *gulag,* in which between 1 and 2 million inmates died, could easily perpetrate such secondary crimes as those against the ethnic Germans. Putin's rule has terrifying antecedents from which, it turns out, it cannot wholly be divorced.

Just how terrifying these antecedents are is demonstrated by perhaps the greatest short and poignant statement about the brutality of the Stalinist regime—which had its roots in Lenin's dictum that the innocent should be persecuted in order to create sheer terror in the population. I am referring to Aleksandr Solzhenitsyn's spare novel *One Day in the Life of Ivan Denisovich,* which chronicles the hour-by-hour experience of an inmate in a Soviet labor camp. "Those who'd come to the end of their time . . . had all been kept in 'pending further orders.' . . . So people originally sentenced to three years did five altogether. They could twist the law any way they liked. When your ten years were up they could say good, have another ten. Or pack you off to some Godforsaken place of exile." Thus does Solzhenitsyn casually reveal how the whole edifice of

Communist ideology rested on utter cynicism. For this is a world where the cracking of one's boots near a fire could doom a man to death in the Siberian winter when the authorities would not give a man a new pair until spring.[10]

Such malice and brutality against innocents rendered the individual utterly meaningless in what for the Soviets was the essentialist struggle between nations and ethnic groups: something that has defined Russian actions through much of history and is a tradition that Putin is heir to. Likewise, wanton destruction and abject cruelty, the bedfellows of indiscipline, combined with bad morale and an historical legacy of seeing flesh-and-blood individuals as mere abstractions that could be wiped off a blackboard, were distinct features of the Russian military in Ukraine, where, as in Stalin's day, cynicism ruled.

Whatever social and political decline has occurred in the United States following the end of the Cold War, the Ukraine War showed Russia—especially as revealed by its war machine—to be in a far more advanced state of rot. The two situations simply cannot be compared. After all, large-scale warfare, with its emphasis, as we know, on materiel, logistics, and social organization, can provide an audit of an entire culture and civilization.[11] In fact, Russian society may actually in some respects have gone backward since the end of the Cold War, since the performance of its military in Afghanistan in the 1980s could arguably be construed as better than in Ukraine. What defeated the Soviet Union in Afghanistan was not really the performance of its troops and logistics, but the sheer task of bringing control and order to an underdeveloped society situated on a sprawling and mountainous landscape. The Soviet military was misused in Afghanistan in a similar way that the U.S. military was misused in both Afghanistan and Iraq. Yes, wars can be audits of whole societies. And warfare showed that Russia in

2022 through 2024 may indeed have gone backward since the days of the old Soviet Union. A Russian victory in Ukraine can only come about through the sheer, brutal application of fresh troops and materiel.

Thus, whereas American politics have struggled to find a new normal after decades of harsh political division, Russian politics, to judge from the audit of the Ukraine War, require rebuilding almost from scratch. In Ukraine, by the end of 2023, Russia had already lost 2,200 out of 3,500 tanks and 315,000 out of 360,000 troops, forcing them to launch recruitment campaigns and raid the prison system. It is as if the entire third-of-a-century since the collapse of the Soviet Union—followed by Boris Yeltsin's shambolic democracy, and then by Putin's more disciplined tyranny—constituted a false start, necessitating another new beginning, as though it were 1991 all over again.

What only the passage of time could reveal in its true enormity was how Russian political culture had been so deformed and debased by the long, morally destructive decades of Communism and especially Stalinism that only a replica of sorts, in this case Putin's style of rule, whose bedrock was utter cynicism much in the tradition of Lenin and Stalin, was possible in the aftermath. To be sure, Vladimir Putin's tyranny demonstrated that the problems of Communism persist in Russia well into the third decade of the 21st century.

In a way, we were all naïve about Communism when the Cold War ended, assuming automatically that Russia and former Communist Central and Eastern Europe could simply cast off their chains and be free. Indeed, Central Europe, which had had a middle-class tradition prior to forty-four years of Communism, had much better prospects than Russia itself, which was largely without such a tradition and had suffered more than seven decades of Communism. The reemergence of a Leninist level of cynicism in the form of Putin's rule, following the chaos of the 1990s, was actually foreseen, albeit indirectly, by the late policy intellectual and former ambassador to the United Nations Jeane J. Kirkpatrick, in her historic and seminal essay "Dictatorships and Double Standards," published in the November 1979 issue of *Commentary*. It is worth spending some time with Kirkpatrick's essay in order to comprehend what we are still up against.

THE FOREIGN POLICY FOLLIES of the Carter Administration were what motivated Kirkpatrick to write her essay. She gets to the point in the first sentence: "The failure of the Carter administration's foreign policy is now clear to everyone except its architects, and even they must entertain certain doubts." The problem, she says, is that President Jimmy Carter behaves like a man who "abhors" only right-wing autocrats, not left-wing ones. And it is the latter, who she defines as "revolutionary," who are the real problem. "Only intellectual fashion and the tyranny of Right/Left thinking prevent intelligent men of good will from perceiving the *facts* that traditional authoritarian governments," that is, right-wing ones, "are less repressive than revolutionary [left-wing] autocracies, that they are more susceptible of liberalization, and that they are more compatible with U.S. interests."

She goes on, and here it is worth quoting her at length:

"Traditional autocrats leave in place existing allocations of wealth, power, status, and other resources which in most traditional societies favor an affluent few and maintain masses in poverty. But they worship traditional gods and observe traditional taboos. They do not disturb the habitual rhythms of work and leisure, habitual places of residence, habitual patterns of family and personal relations." But, she continues, "precisely the opposite is true of revolutionary Communist regimes. They create refugees by the million because they claim jurisdiction over the whole life of society and make demands for change that so violate internalized values and habits that inhabitants flee by the tens of thousands in the remarkable expectation that their attitudes, values, and goals will 'fit' better in a foreign country than in their native land."

Because Kirkpatrick is writing in the late 1970s, her sights are set on the Communist regimes of Asia, particularly Indochina, whose rules sent whole populations into exile. She is also defending the right-wing Somoza regime in Nicaragua and the Shah of Iran, who, despite all their faults, did not seek to reform their societies "in the light of any abstract idea of social justice or political virtue." As we now know, the Nicaraguan Marxists who followed Somoza and the Iranian ayatollahs who followed the Shah did exactly that, and so led their societies into far worse tyrannies, proving Kirkpatrick right.

Kirkpatrick was an original thinker because her philosophy was both realist and neoconservative, which are usually opposed to each other. She was a realist in the sense that she knew that throughout most of history autocracy has been the default option while democracy is problematic. To wit, in Great Britain, the journey from the Magna Carta to the great reform bills took seven centuries to traverse. The United States cannot generally be the "midwife" to democracy far away, she believed. She was a neoconservative during the Cold War because she felt, like President Ronald Reagan did, that the United States had to defeat Communism, not simply coexist with it. Revolutionary Communist regimes destroy societies utterly—by removing all the layers of civic organizations between the regime at the top and the family at the bottom—and thus repairing them, as she likely well understood, would be the project of decades. The debacles of the Yeltsin and Putin regimes in Russia, which followed Communism, again prove her right.

THUS, THE ENDURING LEGACY of Communism (with all of its cynicism) in our world today must be added to the deadly mix encompassing the dystopian uses of technology, the finite size of the earth, the ravages of climate change, the ends of both monarchy and empire, the fast-forward development of precision-guided weaponry as well as of artificial intelligence, and so forth. And this deadly mix also involves the pathologies of urbanization that I will describe in the third part of this book—all in all accounting for the permanent crisis, which, as we will see later on, approximates the inner logic of T. S. Eliot's poem *The Waste Land,* which will take on a new and deeper meaning as the years pass.

IMAGINE, PUTIN HAD LOOKED so powerful, well-nigh invincible, on the eve of his invasion of Ukraine on February 23, 2022, with his armies massed on three of Ukraine's borders, poised to advance. NATO at this moment was still divided, with the Germans and French adopting a softer approach than the Poles, Balts, and other Central and Eastern Europeans who actually share borders with Russia. And Russian natural gas was ruling the roost, as it had done for years. The memory of Putin's victories in the small wars of the turn of the 21st century was still fresh. Putin at this moment in time was grudgingly respected as a formidable tactician. His annexation of Crimea and military subversion of eastern Ukraine in 2014 were popular at home, even as they angered Western policy elites. But, like the wars in the Balkans in the 1990s, they did not pivotally engage larger American and European publics, so that we can say Putin got away with it here, too. History often rests on a pivot. It is not all about vast impersonal forces but often about the emotions of an individual leader. And such a choice as Putin had to make was binary in the extreme, even as he faced a situation on the ground in Ukraine that appeared murky and given to mysteries. Would the Ukrainians quickly surrender? Or would they fight back hard?

Had Putin not invaded and instead negotiated Ukraine's neutrality from a position of strength, Russia would likely still be perceived as a daunting great power. But as he chose to send columns of tanks racing across the border, his army and the weaponry it carried, and the culture that both encapsulated, were quickly exposed as simply not of first-world quality, and were thus at first easily countered by NATO's arms deliveries to the Ukrainians. In fact, what followed, given the fighting spirit of the Ukrainians and the tens of billions of dollars' worth of military equipment that the Biden Administration dispatched to Ukraine, was the greatest demonstration of American power since the First Gulf War of 1991, when the United States ejected Iraqi forces from Kuwait under President George H. W. Bush. Suddenly, America loomed like a giant over the hapless Russians, who would soon be throwing hundreds of thousands of raw, barely trained conscripts into battle to gain a few inches or feet of territory. Russia would recover, sure, and fight the Ukrainians to a standstill, and even outlast them. But would the Russian Empire—that is, Russia's profound influence in the North and Trans Caucasus, in Central Asia, Siberia, and the Far East—ultimately be able to withstand the enormous diversion of resources to the Ukraine War? World War I changed the 20th century and the world because it went on for four years. Had it gone on for only a year, or maybe two, the destruction would have been mitigated, Lenin perhaps would not have come to power, and neither might Hitler later on. Thus, every extra month of continued fighting in Ukraine might affect Russia and its imperial project similarly, to say nothing of its effect on the world.

In the decades prior to World War I, the European powers were preoccupied with the so-called Eastern Question, which was about how to respond to the slow-motion demise of the Ottoman Empire, whose cruelty was "tempered only by incompetence."[12] The same could be said about the Russians in Ukraine. And likewise, the Eastern Question may again be on the table, as the United States and Europe spend the years to come dealing with the demise or transformation of the Russian Empire.

Once again, American decline was in relative terms subtle and qualitative, with both major political parties at times gravitating toward the extremes, with racial tensions periodically on the boil, with cultural standards in disarray, with the liberal arts that educate new generations of Americans threatened by ideology, and so forth. But Russia's civilizational decline was fundamental and quantitative: it simply had no usable institutions, no system of leadership replacement even. The state was a force of nature best to be avoided whenever possible. The initial failure of the army was obviously reflective of the whole Russian state in this regard, starting at the top where no one dared to tell Putin the truth. Which was the ultimate reason he had such a difficult time at the beginning achieving victory in Ukraine. That is the chief problem with authoritarian leaders. The very intimidating nature of their rule makes it difficult for subordinates to risk a confrontation with the boss, and thus the very anxious foresight based on unpleasant facts—precisely the facts required for difficult decisions—is harder than usual to come by. Authoritarian leaders like Vladimir Putin and Xi Jinping are, to some extent, operating blind. And because of their enormous power over events, they endanger not just their own countries but the whole world as a consequence. Democracies can be undynamic, late to the party, and weak in decision-making. But in their consultative ways they have generally less of a capacity for outright blunders than authoritarians do. Yes, the democratically elected younger Bush invaded Iraq. But Putin committed the larger blunder of invading Ukraine, Stalin decimated his officer corps before World War II, and Hitler invaded the Soviet Union. The list of self-defeating blunders made by dictators is much longer than those of democrats. A world where major powers are governed by authoritarians is, therefore, that much more unstable. Authoritarians ruling Russia, China, Iran, and so on are another element of our permanent crisis. They provide order, but of an extremely uncertain kind.

Putin's eventual downfall will more likely lead to anarchy than to stable democracy, or more likely to a messy and ill-defined political situation in Russia. We should keep Russia's semi-anarchic situation in the 1990s in mind given what may follow in the coming years. The perils of post-autocracy are real. Like empires, autocrats often arise out of chaos but also leave chaos in their wake. Communism, which as a morally debased political culture continued in spirit unabated under Putin, has left no sustainable institutions to work within. Because Jeane Kirkpatrick's analysis of the difference between right- and left-wing dictatorships was correct, and has admirably stood the test of time, we must be patient regarding Russia. As Daniel Patrick Moynihan reminded us, the central conservative truth is the preeminence of culture, not politics, in determining the success of a society. In Russia's case, the damage of over a century of extreme misrule on the culture will not be wiped clean in a week or a year even. To repeat: just as 19th-century European diplomats faced the Eastern Question brought about by the weakening of Ottoman Turkey, 21st-century Western diplomats will face the Eurasian Question, brought about by the potential weakening and tumultuous transition of Russia.

IN ADDITION TO RUSSIAN and American decline, there is also the Chinese variety.

For decades China often seemed invincible to Americans, the very engine of economic and technological growth that has transformed both itself and the world. No nation in recorded economic history has improved the standard of living and the quality of life of so many people as quickly as China has under the extraordinary rule of Deng Xiaoping and his immediate successors.

Deng has often been underrated in the West. When the last century ended, American pundits and intellectuals were divided over whether Winston Churchill, Franklin D. Roosevelt, or Albert Einstein was the greatest man of the past hundred years. The name of Deng Xiaoping, China's ruler, official and de facto, from the mid-1970s to the early 1990s, was barely mentioned. That reflected a classic Western mindset, concerned with its own historical experience rather than with that of others, and which sees freedom in political and philosophical terms more than in social and economic terms. But given what is relevant for our own time—a time of instability, destructive populism, intemperate dictatorships, and anarchy in places—in light of the struggles of silent billions across the planet who worry about putting enough food on the table and providing safety for their families more than they worry about the right to vote, Deng's accomplishment is the greater. Deng is what is missing in today's global environment. The absence of his likeness contributes to the permanent crisis. It may be too much to expect that great powers like China and Russia be both stable and democratic. It would be enough that they be stable and ruled by leaders who are both enlightened and bureaucratically competent. Therefore, I want to spend some time with Harvard professor Ezra Vogel's magisterial biography of Deng Xiaoping, who more than any other man was the father of the original Asian economic miracle, and whose story reads as though taken from the pages of Plutarch's *Lives of the Noble Greeks and Romans*.

DENG TOOK OVER CHINA in the shadow of Mao Zedong. Mao had left China a social, institutional, and economic wreck. The country of 1 billion people at the time had been plunged into chaos. Universities had closed. Educated youth were forced into rural exile, even as the cities had no jobs for them. Soldiers and party cadres with no bureaucratic experience controlled the ministries. Eighty percent of the population lived on $40 per year. This all constituted the immediate aftermath of Mao's Great Proletarian Cultural Revolution.

Enter Deng Xiaoping.

Ezra Vogel writes that "some Westerners were so impressed with Deng's directness and pragmatism that they mistakenly thought he was a capitalist at heart and that he would lead China toward a Western-style democracy." But Deng knew better what was good for China, "and it was not capitalism and . . . democracy," according to Vogel. "In the process, stepping stone by stepping stone, he guided the transformation of China into a country that was scarcely recognizable from the one he had inherited in 1978." At first, Deng rebuilt the Communist party from the chaos of the Cultural Revolution because he knew that only the Communist party, with all of its faults, could provide order at that moment.[13] The Americans had applied this lesson when they granted amnesty to the rank-and-file of the Nazi party in occupied Germany after World War II in order to get Germany back on its feet, but forgot it when they completely disbanded the Ba'ath party in Iraq following the occupation of that country in 2003.

Deng's good sense was a product of his life experience. In his mid-twenties, in Guangxi, in south-central China, he led Communist troops and militia in pitched battles against nationalists. He experienced the death of his wife and infant child on account of a miscarriage during feverish conditions in a local hospital. He then fought the Japanese invaders, and decided on executions during intense factional infighting. He struggled to construct a political order in his patch of ground rather than make an existing one less oppressive—only to be purged by Mao and endure hard labor and reeducation in the provinces. During the Cultural Revolution, Deng Pufang, Deng's son by his third wife, was paralyzed by falling from a third-floor window while being tortured by Red Guards. Deng resolved to keep praising Mao and keep him on a pedestal, but to bravely adapt party strategy to new and changing conditions. In the mid-1970s, while in the process of achieving power, Deng took the military out of party positions and returned it to the barracks. He promoted cadres based on talent and competence rather than on ideology. He knew that stability preceded modernization, and did his best to undermine hero worship, hardline ideology, and mass mobilization, the very opposite of Mao and China's current ruler, Xi Jinping. "Deng would not tolerate the cult of personality that Mao happily indulged in," writes Vogel; "virtually no statues of Deng were placed in public buildings and virtually no pictures of him hung in homes."[14]

Deng's crucial decision, which has determined his status as a great historical figure, was his introduction of elements of capitalism into Communist China gradually, rather than through shock therapy as the Russians under American guidance attempted. He knew, writes Vogel, that "China did not have the experience, rules, knowledgeable entrepreneurs, or private capital needed to convert suddenly to a market economy."[15] Because Deng lived in constant fear of chaos, he managed to avoid it, while reinventing China at the same time. He was in his own way a Burkean conservative, seeking the preservation of existing systems and values while concomitantly forcing them to evolve. He opted for gradual economic change and chose party reform, with term limits, over the introduction of democracy. Thus did China become a role model for the developing world.

Nevertheless, Deng, at eighty-four, remained the final decision-maker in the government crackdown against student-led demonstrations at Tiananmen Square in June 1989, when hundreds if not thousands were killed. The students had wanted more sudden, democratic change. Yet, as Vogel notes, "in the two decades after Tiananmen, China enjoyed relative stability and rapid—even spectacular—economic growth."[16] China's trade with the world increased a hundredfold, and 1.4 million young Chinese went abroad to study. Much of that was either under Deng or the result of policies that Deng had put in place. And much of that, too, was in the wake of Tiananmen, not before.

The difference between the world situation then and now, and between U.S.-China relations then and now, is the difference between Deng Xiaoping and Xi Jinping. Deng, in keeping with his concentration on developing the Chinese economy and improving the daily life of average Chinese citizens, did not provoke tensions abroad, preferring trade to conflict, unlike Xi. The world has become what it is to a significant extent because we have autocrats like Xi and Putin holding sway rather than Deng and Gorbachev. The last decades of the 20th century were eras of hope in American-Chinese relations because they coincided with the era of Deng and his like-minded successors. As for the decline in U.S. presidential leadership, it has been real, but minor, compared to the decline in Chinese and Russian leadership, where pragmatism has given way to Leninist ideology in Beijing and to Great Russian imperialism in Moscow.

XI JINPING IS NOTHING if not a Leninist ideologue, who has made "struggle" the guiding principle of the Chinese Communist party. In speeches to top party leaders that were kept secret for months before being released in Chinese, Xi denounced the fall of the Soviet Union, and said that "to dismiss Lenin and Stalin . . . is to engage in historic nihilism: it confuses our thoughts and undermines the Party's organization on all levels." Xi has lamented the failure of the 1991 attempt by Soviet hardliners to topple Mikhail Gorbachev: "Nobody was man enough to stand up and resist." Xi goes on, "Facts have repeatedly told us that Marx and Engels' analysis of the basic contradiction of capitalist society is not outdated, nor is the historical materialist view that capitalism will inevitably perish and socialism will inevitably triumph outdated."[17]

For Xi, absolute power and absolute commitment to Leninist ideology with its focus on pure dictatorship in a one-party state is not enough. To punctuate his return of China to pure Maoist principles, derivative of Lenin, someone very prominent had to be publicly humiliated in a dramatic fashion in order to drive the point home. Thus, Xi's consolidation of power at the Communist party congress in October 2022 in Beijing was accomplished with a cruel personal twist. Hu Jintao, Xi's predecessor as president and the previous boss of China, seated next to Xi, appeared to be forcibly removed from the closing session of the congress by two attendants and perp-walked before the television cameras. Hu was the last in the line of moderate and pragmatic party leaders stemming from Deng. And his involuntary departure from the hall symbolized the end of an era, and signaled that the world would be more dangerous going forward.

Indeed, Xi emerged from the party congress with a grip on power unrivaled since Mao. And thus his ability to make big mistakes that could shake the world is also unrivaled. His decision not to import foreign vaccines, coupled with China's sudden exit from a zero-Covid regimen, could still have serious international health consequences. His drive for state control will produce arbitrary economic decisions and policy instability, affecting us all, according to Eurasia Group, a New York–based risk consultancy. Vladimir Putin gave us the Ukraine War. We should be wary of Xi Jinping giving the world something perhaps just as deadly in China's own, highly sophisticated way. For China operates at a higher level than did Russia or the former Soviet Union.

WHEREAS DURING THE COLD WAR the Soviet Union represented a credible adversary in niche capacities only—nuclear weapons, conventional land warfare, manned space exploration—China competes credibly with America across the board. China is a full-spectrum economic and military power with a vast first-world navy, nuclear weapons, a strengthening NCO corps, and cyber and digital capacities that carry over from the military to the consumer sphere. China is preparing to send a man to the moon. Its efficient assembly-line workers manufacture many of the sophisticated electronics that America and the world take for granted. Because of all these successes, and because of its somewhat opaque authoritarianism, China's political stability has been for too long taken for granted. But China, like the United States and Russia, though in varying degrees, is in decline. As we know, the rules of Deng Xiaoping, Jiang Zemin, and Hu Jintao signified a relatively progressive, enlightened, and collegial authoritarianism that Americans and Europeans—particularly Western businessmen—were comfortable with. This period saw China at the peak of its soft power, to say nothing of its hard power, as China had friends in Washington: not only in the business community but actually in the media, Congress, and the White House as well. But, this comfort/bonhomie belies the fact that Xi Jinping has returned China to the die-hard authoritarianism, bordering on totalitarianism, associated with Mao Zedong. As a consequence, China has lost almost all its friends in Washington.

While this has been happening, China's annual economic growth has been slowing from double digits down to single digits, and finally perhaps to low single digits. Capital has fled the country, with foreign investors selling many billions of dollars in Chinese bonds and billions more in Chinese stocks. At the same time that China's economy has matured and investment from abroad has diminished, its population has aged and its workforce has shrunk, with reduced economic growth the consequence. Moreover, by directing economic activity and decision-making increasingly to the state, Xi Jinping, according to Kevin Rudd, the global president of the Asia Society, "has been strangling the goose" that for almost four decades "has laid the golden egg."[18] And as China's declining economy leads to more social and political tensions—look at the demonstrations in late 2022 against the Covid-19 lockdown—the default option for its leaders may well be a greater dose of self-righteous nationalism and foreign policy assertiveness. Keep in mind that the Pentagon projects China will have at least 1,000 nuclear weapons by the end of the decade.[19] Thus, here as in Russia, the problems of Communism are still with us, and as a consequence, military tensions remain high in the Western Pacific.

To wit, Japan will be increasing its defense budget by over 50 percent in coming years, as well as acquiring hundreds of advanced missiles that can reach far into China and North Korea, which Japan now sees as active threats. The Japanese are particularly alarmed by the prospect of a Chinese invasion of Taiwan, which is close to their own Ryukyu Islands. Meanwhile, as Xi's China has forced Japan out of its pacifist shell and made it further enlarge its already robust navy and air force, the United States, Great Britain, and Australia have embarked on a military-industrial policy to provide Australia with nuclear-powered submarines that it can operate close to China. Just as Britain has served since before World War II as a geopolitical platform for the United States close to mainland Europe, Australia, situated at the confluence of the Pacific and Indian oceans, will henceforth do the same for the Indo-Pacific region close to mainland China. This new, de facto Anglo-Saxon alliance effectively joins NATO to the Indo-Pacific through Great Britain, and specifically links NATO to "the Quad," the Indo-Pacific alliance of democracies that includes Japan and India as well as the United States and Australia.[20] This, again, is an example of the destabilizing effect of a finite earth as military alliance systems now operate as a unified whole in both hemispheres, and on both ends of the Eurasian super-continent. Whereas in World War II, the European and Pacific theaters were more or less separate, in the 21st century the linkages between the two theaters will be much more organic, as Europe itself is becoming more of a player in Pacific defense, in addition to its robust economic links with China. The globe is becoming the worst of both worlds: a unified theater of conflict, but one where each far-flung extremity of that theater can tweak the other end thousands of miles away and cause an eruption.

This new cold war between the United States and China is not likely to end for the foreseeable future, barring some unforeseen development. The United States and China are at odds on several major fronts. The Chinese military sees the South and East China seas as its home territory; the blue-water extensions of its continental landmass, much as the Americans saw the Caribbean in the late 19th and early 20th centuries. On the other hand, the U.S. military sees the Western Pacific as its home waters, too, believing that the United States is an Asian power going all the way back to the 1853 opening of Japan, the Philippine War at the turn of the 20th century, World War II in the Pacific, Korea, and Vietnam. The cyber age only makes this conflict more tense, as the enemy is now one click away rather than thousands of miles away, with the ability of a computer to wreak destruction from afar. The Chinese have already launched major hacking operations against the Pentagon and the U.S. Navy. A future war in the Pacific would be a contest of computerized and artificial intelligence—driven weapons systems linking warships and outer space. Then there is trade, where the two countries are in a tense competition, even as they cooperate. Perhaps never before in modern history have two major powers been on the brink of conflict yet so entangled in mutually beneficial economic relations. This is the biggest factor distinguishing the present cold war from the one with the Soviet Union, which essentially had no trading and manufacturing economy. And it is also intrinsic to an era of globalization and regionalization on a finite earth, in which states are tightly interlinked on multiple levels, even as they compete. Finally, there is ideology, which we have covered by comparing Deng Xiaoping with Xi Jinping. When China was led by more moderate leaders, there was still a profound difference between its system and our own democratic one. But now under Xi's totalitarianism the difference between it and the United States is that much *harder:* there is a total philosophical clash of systems of governance. And with that comes mutual animosity and suspicion, in which every dispute is imagined as existential.

The best that can be hoped for in this cold war between the United States and China is a condition akin to that after the Cuban Missile Crisis. During the Cuban Missile Crisis of 1962, both superpowers stared into the abyss, palpably seeing the possibility of all-out nuclear war. Because such a specter completely terrified them, they henceforth stepped back, and over the coming years established a "hot line" between the American and Soviet leaders, designed to facilitate communication, and initialed various kinds of treaties meant to limit the possibility of nuclear conflict, all of which culminated in détente. The issues of the Cold War weren't solved, but rules of the road were built around them. This happened even as the Soviet Union had quietly begun to decline, though few were then aware of it.

CHINA, TOO, IS IN decline, with a population aging at a faster rate than America's (it is shrinking, actually) and with its complex economy directed by Marxist-Leninist ideologues. Because all three great powers—Russia, China, and the United States—are in decline, though in different ways and at different rates, it may be that the United States, which maintains the capacity for democratic renewal, has a comparative advantage over the two authoritarian powers, despite its soaring deficit.

It is also important to realize that each great power, again in its own way, is an imperial one. Russian historical imperialism (going back to the conquests of the Romanov dynasty) was obviously evident in Ukraine. Chinese historical imperialism (going back at least to the conquest of the Qing dynasty) is evident in its longing to rule Taiwan. As for the United States, since the end of World War II, given its globe-spanning economic and military power, it has been an empire in all but name. Thus, the decline of the great powers signals another death knell for the stabilizing virtues of imperialism and the relative political order it brings—which go back to the dawn of history, however out of fashion imperialism has been since the second half of the 20th century.

But, because the declines of the three great powers are relative to one another, there will be twists and turns in this process. For example, because Russia is declining at a faster rate than China, China's leverage over Russia has increased. This has led to Russia becoming a sphere of Chinese influence, as China extracts hydrocarbons from Russia at bargain-basement prices, overwhelms Russian influence in former Soviet Central Asia, and so forth. China, in other words, because of Russia's weakening position, has gone from being a Pacific and Asian power to becoming a *Eurasian* one. For most of history the super-continent of Eurasia was too big to have any graspable meaning. But as I wrote in *The Revenge of Geography* (2012) and *The Return of Marco Polo's World* (2018), the very shrinkage of the earth through geography has created a situation where Eurasia is suddenly imaginable in geopolitical terms. China's emergence as a *Eurasian* power, encompassing Russia, is only an early sign of this.[21]

ONCE MORE, EMPIRES ARISE out of chaos but their weakening and dissolution give way to new forms of chaos. History grants no solution to this dilemma. Imperial decline can take years, decades, or even centuries, all the while leading to regional turmoil and other pathologies. The Ottoman Empire was famously the "sick man of Europe" throughout much of the 19th and early 20th centuries, culminating in the Balkan Wars, World War I, and the Greco-Turkish War. Because the decline of imperial powers can mean more aggression on their part (as they become more insecure and desperate), even as there is increased chaos in their shadowlands, global geopolitics will become more tumultuous, not less. To use a financial term, we will for the foreseeable future be in a geopolitical bear market.

Let me emphasize: the second- and third-order effects of great-power decline, however gradual and uneven, will mean more outrages in the developing world and in the international system. Areas previously thought of as relatively stable will become less so. Disequilibria everywhere will intensify.

Europe's stability will continue to be undermined by Russia. A post-Putin age in Moscow could be just as dangerous as the current condition. Russia is a weakly institutionalized state, especially compared to China, in which a form of anarchy could easily follow Putin. In terms of potential disarray, Russia might even become a low-calorie version of the former Yugoslavia, a crumbling state with enough nuclear weapons to destroy the United States in thirty minutes. There is no agreed-upon procedure to replace Putin, unlike in China, where the Communist party has a procedure to replace Xi should he become incapacitated. Putin himself will have to rule until his death to be safe, and that was the situation even before he invaded Ukraine. Putin is at the center of several branches and circles of oligarchs and military and intelligence strongmen, who have all relied on him for their power and positions. That is the true extent of Russia's executive branch. Thus, a stable democracy is not the *base case* scenario for Russia after Putin. The *base case* scenario is something akin to a militarist-nationalist regime, or a democracy too incoherent to be able to actually govern. That will lead to more anarchy and instability in the weakly institutionalized regions of the Russian Empire, even as China gains a stronger foothold there. Because such places are not in the forefront of the minds of the Washington and New York elites, they will pay it little heed, even as they proclaim an age of democracy because of the eventual rebuilding of postwar Ukraine.

A victorious, postwar Ukraine would formally or informally be incorporated into NATO and the EU, bodily moving the original Atlantic Alliance with its economic equivalent eastward. Even under the best of circumstances, that would be a lot to digest for the bureaucrats in Brussels. Ukraine is a war-battered country of 44 million people with fragile institutions and a high level of corruption. Absorbing Iberia, Greece, and Turkey into NATO and Iberia and Greece into the EU were never easy challenges; nor was the later incorporation of former Communist Central Europe and parts of the Balkans. In the mid- and late 2020s, this enlarged and sprawling NATO and EU will be preoccupied with their newest member. And that will lead to informal constellations within those organizations. The bigger an organization becomes, often the more unwieldy and superficial it becomes, changing its very nature, as we have learned from many a corporate merger. NATO could informally divide into a more militant Poland-Ukraine-Romania axis, supported by Great Britain, and replicating the old Intermarium, a 1920s concept meaning "between the seas," the Baltic and Black seas, that is—a belt of states to guard against Russian expansion westward. Such a subdivision of NATO, which might weaken the Alliance overall, would compete with a more pacifistic France and Germany, while Sweden, Finland, and the three former Soviet-Baltic states created their own nervous security system to guard against Russia, which even in a state of post-Putin weakness and disorder will be nuclear-armed and dangerous, and with a long history of rebuilding its empire from bouts of chaos. Then there will be the Mediterranean countries of NATO and the EU, which will naturally concentrate on the problem of refugees and migrants coming from the higher-birth-rate areas of Africa and the Middle East through the course of the 21st century. The populations of Africa and the Middle East will increase from 1.7 billion people to 4.4 billion by the end of this century, while Europe's indigenous population rate remains stagnant.[22] In Africa, 95 percent of the labor force depends on informal employment, which is why tens of millions and more want to migrate northward.[23] No, Europe will not be altogether stable. It might turn out that along with long periods of the 19th century, between the Napoleonic Wars and World War I, the Cold War division of the second half of the 20th century will continue to stand as Europe's most tranquil epoch.

As for Asia, we know that its stability will be undermined by the shock effects of a rapidly arming, more nationalist and tumultuous China under Leninist rule. That will naturally mean higher defense budgets and greater naval activity throughout the Western Pacific and Indian Ocean. Such competition will be both abstract and alienating, as thousands of officers and sailors labor under grim lighting, conducting operations through computer screens inside gray-hulled warships, where war games are just as tense as live fire drills on land, as I can attest as an embedded journalist on destroyers and submarines. The chances of actual military conflict in the South and East China seas will be quite small, but if it should happen the consequences for financial markets will be severe, far more severe than the market reaction to the Ukraine and Middle East wars, as the world's three largest economies will be at loggerheads with high-end weaponry. Meanwhile, North Korea periodically threatens conflagration against not just South Korea, but against Japan and the United States, too, as deliverable nuclear weapons remain its best real defense against any attempts at regime change.

The Middle East will continue in its struggle to create regimes, democratic or not, that avoid tyranny on one hand and anarchy on the other. This will become more rather than less difficult as populations in the Middle East increase in absolute terms, even as the underground water table continues to gradually diminish. This losing battle could lead to environmental *hard* regimes, Hobbesian in nature, as exist in Egypt, whose autocratic and paranoid style is ultimately the result of it having no answers to the question of people versus natural resources, aggravated by climate change. Pakistan may be the most extreme example of this approaching phenomenon: an artificially conceived country where democracy has never worked amid resource scarcity, vast corruption, unruly shantytowns and mega-cities, and ethnic and sectarian strife, each category working against the others to create ungovernability.

Of course, this more or less describes quite a number of sub-Saharan countries, too. We are told that because of Africa's relatively high population growth rate, along with its enlarging middle class, the 21st century will triumphantly be an African one. The fact that African countries fill the lower and lowest ranks of the United Nations' Human Development Index for reasons directly related to such a high population growth rate is rarely mentioned. (The bottom ten countries on the index are all in sub-Saharan Africa.) As I have said earlier, Africa will constitute 40 percent of the world population by 2100. We are indeed entering a world that will be vast yet claustrophobic, more reachable yet more intractable and complicated, and most important, less and less tempered by the great powers, which will have no solutions for many countries.

NEVERTHELESS, AT THE MOMENT that I write, geopolitics has a very particular tendency. Let me explain.

A worldwide, bipolar military conflict has begun. It will progress in stages, feature hot war in certain places for extended periods of time, and cold war in other places and times. It will be the organizing principle of geopolitics for a few years to come. It is not a "clash of civilizations," as Samuel Huntington put it, but it is a *clash:* a clash of broad value systems, which, while having their roots in national cultures and age-old traditions, are essentially modern and postmodern in their origins. It is a bipolar struggle that fuses the Global War on Terrorism with great-power conflict. Rather than the latter replacing the former as many had supposed would occur following the conclusion of our post-9/11 Mideast wars and Russia's 2022 invasion of Ukraine, the two dramas now run together—as a result of the Gaza War and the mass casualty terror attacks it may yet spawn.

One pole of this bipolar world features gangster states like Russia and North Korea; totalitarian states like China and, again, North Korea; a revolutionary and terrorist state like clerical Iran, with all of its proxies; and a movement that, as I shall explain, is at once age-old, Industrial, and post-Industrial: anti-Semitism. These are enemies more formidable and in ways more nihilistic than the old Soviet Union and Mao Zedong's China. The Soviet leaders, who, because they were in many cases survivors of World War II and Stalin's purges, were generally conservative and risk-averse in their actions. And when they weren't, like Nikita Khrushchev in the 1962 Cuban Missile Crisis, they paid the price by being ousted from power. Leonid Brezhnev's 1979 invasion of Afghanistan led eventually to the collapse of the Soviet system altogether. As for Mao, with all of his atrocities against his own people, he could be a rational actor in foreign affairs, as the Nixon Administration demonstrated. The current crop of villains constitute a more unstable, harder-to-predict human element than what we were used to dealing with during the Cold War.

And these villains are all interlocked.

Russia, through its Wagner mercenary group, threatened to send an air defense system to help the Iranian proxy Hezbollah fight Israel on the Israel-Lebanon border. Russia's new military alliance with Iran, which garners materiel and drones for Moscow in its war against Ukraine, makes President Vladimir Putin a de facto ally of Iranian supreme leader Ali Khamenei against Israel. North Korea is also sending arms to Russia, which helps Russia in its invasion of Ukraine, even as China backs Russia and benefits from the distraction of Hamas's attack on Israel. This is how the Ukraine and Gaza wars are connected.

In all of this, we should be careful how we label our own side. Our side would be wrongly labeled as the world of democracies, not only because something such as anti-Semitism has rooted itself inside democracies themselves (witness our university campuses), but because our own side also includes conservative autocracies such as the regimes in the Arabian Gulf, Jordan, Egypt, and elsewhere, which stand for the regional status quo, as opposed to the revolutionary chaos that a regime like Iran threatens to bring about. In fact, this is a bipolar struggle between status quo powers like ourselves and leaders and movements that want to topple the existing post–Cold War order, whether by territorial acquisition like Russia in Ukraine, or like China in regard to Taiwan, or by the eradication of an entire people—the goal of Iran's coalition regarding Israel. Order versus disorder. That is what it's about. World War II was similar, since the Nazis and Japanese fascists attempted to replace an orderly world, with all of its faults, with revolutionary mass murder, military conquest, and extremism. Our Cold War adversaries were cautious by comparison.

In geopolitical terms, the struggle is also between the Eurasian Heartland powers of Russia, China, North Korea, and Iran, and the Rimland powers that are essentially maritime, with some variations, such as the United States, Europe, Ukraine, Israel, and the conservative Sunni Arab powers from the Gulf to the Red Sea and the Mediterranean. These are geographical distinctions about which I wrote at length in *The Revenge of Geography*. But I must admit, given how technology has compressed geography, creating through digital media a global platform for performance politics, this is better understood as a war of ideas with geopolitical and military ramifications. The Heartland and Rimland divisions just don't capture the flavor of what is happening. Anti-Semitism does: since in its latest iteration it has been ignited by the war between Israel and Gaza and has since spread throughout the West, to the Russian Empire, and to China. Witness the pogrom-like riot in the Russian republic of Dagestan in response to the arrival of a flight from Israel, and the attacks on Jews in Chinese social-media circles in the wake of Hamas's October 7, 2023, attack.

Anti-Semitism is a word with deep historical associations. It conjures up hatred of Jews in medieval Europe and pogroms against Jews in Russia's Pale of Settlement before and around the turn of the 20th century, and, of course, it culminates in the Nazi Holocaust in the mid-20th century. The Holocaust, in particular, gave anti-Semitism an Industrial Age aura, with converging railway tracks as a signature of both the Industrial Age and of trains transporting Jews to death camps. But anti-Semitism can be post-Industrial, too, with its own new associations, even when wrapped around a territorial dispute between Israelis and Palestinians, as when Hamas terrorists used GoPro cameras to record their slaughter of Jewish women, children, and elderly people on October 7th. That was nihilism, violent Jew-hatred, postmodern performance politics, and Iranian grand strategy all at once, with clear-cut benefits to Russia and China.

Israel stands at the heart of this global geopolitical war. That is because Israel hasn't really wavered. Israel is not the Biden Administration giving the Ukrainians just enough aid and weaponry to wear down the Russians, but not enough to win outright. It is not Chinese president Xi Jinping biding his time about if and when to make a dramatic move to undermine Taiwan's de facto independence. It is not even Iran, which possibly seeks all the benefits of being a threshold nuclear power without actually using a bomb. Israel, although its population may be divided on many issues, is absolutely united about the need to militarily defend its territory, to defeat Hamas, and to neutralize Iran and its proxies.

Ultimately, the shadow war between Israel and Iran—Israel's industrial sabotage, its assassination of Iranian nuclear scientists—may ignite into a full-scale conflict with Israel frontally attacking Iran. I advance this theory mainly because the very intimacy and horror of October 7th, in which 1,200 Israelis were killed, tortured, raped, and kidnapped in the most hideous manner, may have shifted Israeli calculations about Iran—Hamas's principal backer—in a more decisive direction.

Beyond this, many scenarios are possible. Keep in mind that clerical rule in Iran rests on an increasingly narrow base of support. Iran has been likened to a country of 85 million South Koreans ruled by a clique of North Koreans. Vast anti-government demonstrations, calling for the downfall of the ayatollahs, occurred in 2022. And they were not the first: 2009, 2017, 2018, and 2019 also saw massive anti-regime uprisings. It is a long way from such large protests to true political upheaval. But it was massive protests that toppled the Shah's regime in 1979. We have to be able to imagine a post-revolutionary system in Iran, or at least the kind of instability that starts to immobilize the current power structure. An event from outside, such as a successful Israeli or Israeli-American attack on Iranian nuclear and missile facilities may help to do just that.

As for the Ukraine War, as I've said, it may just be a curtain-raiser for ugly unrest elsewhere across the sprawling Russian Empire, where Siberian republics such as Buryatia and Tuva have provided troops for Ukraine, and have died in proportionally much greater numbers than ethnic Russians from places like Moscow and St. Petersburg. The Russian Empire, as this war in Ukraine grinds on, may be ready to start crumbling.

AND CURIOUSLY, SUCH A world will be less and less understood, as frightful headlines and imperfect media accounts from distant places take precedence over what is actually happening on the ground, not only in Russia and the Middle East, but in sprawling cities, slums, and roads in the bush. That is the realm we enter next: the realm of our own Western consciousness as it plunges into the crosscurrents of other consciousnesses and civilizations, nevertheless struggling to survive and both influence and direct all those colliding geopolitical forces mentioned above. Isolationism is the past: full immersion in a chaotic world is the inevitable future.

III.

CROWDS AND CHAOS

THE FUNDAMENTAL CHANGE IN GEOPOLITICS HAS NOT BEEN FULLY realized. Great-power divides, the collapse of empires, the shrinkage of geography through technology, the legacy of Communism, and Shakespearean decline all play monumental roles in the roiling instability of our world. But there is something at once broader and more subtle that affects both world politics and our daily lives.

In fact, the primary change in geopolitics is urbanization, and the intensification of politics that it leads to. Over 55 percent of humanity lives in cities, by 2050 over two-thirds of humanity will be urban, and increasingly *densely* urban. In 1975 there were only three mega-cities with populations in the tens of millions (Tokyo, New York, and Mexico City). By 2014 there were thirty-four such cities.[1] This is a primary change because while great-power fractures affect foreign affairs on a surface level, urbanization combined with social media provides the psychological and cultural undercurrents that drive foreign affairs from below the surface, making international politics more turbulent. So I need to describe it.

Perhaps nobody in the 20th century understood cities on a human level—what made them work, what made them not work, and what they originally were supposed to be—like the late American Canadian journalist Jane Jacobs, author of the masterpiece *The Death and Life of Great American Cities*. Jacobs cut through all the theory and jargon to announce that it was all about sidewalks; not scale, not how tall or beautiful the buildings were: "If a city's streets look interesting, the city looks interesting; if they look dull, the city looks dull." Unlike towns and outlying suburbs, "cities are, by definition, full of strangers." And it is the effect of one stranger upon another, and one store upon another and upon each pedestrian, that, Jacobs explains, determines the success or failure of a city. "Lowly, unpurposeful and random as they may appear, sidewalk contacts are the small change from which a city's wealth of public life may grow." Neighborhoods, and by extension sidewalks, require people of different income groups to function and interact with each other, she implied.

Of course, nowadays too many cities and downtowns (at least during the daytime) are for the wealthy, and for people who are all alike rather than different, resulting in what Jacobs prophetically calls the "Great Blight of Dullness." Indeed, everyone in wealthy districts thinks of themselves as just so fascinating, and dresses accordingly, that in straining to be unique they are all actually the same. Jacobs says that it is "differences, *not duplications*" that make for well-functioning and truly aesthetic cities. But too often the result is "monotony," in which one city, and one part of town along with its inhabitants, almost exactly resembles another. And because, over the years and decades, as wealth has poured into American cities, resulting in new and glitzier buildings, only the chain stores and restaurants can afford the rents, adding another layer of dullness.[2] This has especially been the case with American cities, which "came into being as places where people could make money," unlike European and Asian ones, which were founded as centers of culture and political power, explain the urbanists Dennis R. Judd and Todd Swanstrom.[3]

Cities, not just in America but all over the world, glittering and monochrome, with traffic jams everywhere, have grown in such scale, anchoring our very tightening global system, that Jacobs's comments about sidewalks and neighborhoods may seem quaint, however necessary they still are. In fact, Jacobs's observations easily apply to cities all over the world, which can be dull or interesting depending upon the factors she describes. Indeed, cities were never tidy and picturesque, as Jacobs well knew. They were always difficult places. In almost the same year that Jacobs published her monumental and hopeful book, the poet Robert Lowell detected a "savage servility" beginning to overtake formerly genteel Boston.[4] Decades earlier, in fact, the critic Edmund Wilson was struck by "people grinding at barren office-routine in the cells of gigantic cities."[5] And in the mid-19th century, the Scottish essayist Thomas Carlyle saw in the crowds of London a vision of maggots teeming in cheese.[6] That was the London that served as a spiritual backdrop for much of Charles Dickens's famously harsh fiction about the human condition.

Jacobs was not oblivious to any of this. The city for her was a *project,* a place that could be made to work. She saw in successful cities places where opinions might be different but people could still get along, as a result of civic pride and politeness. That was the whole point. What she did not see, because she wrote in the middle and latter part of the 20th century, before there was the merging of digital platforms with city life, and henceforth the monumental effect of social media on city life, was how cities, rather than places of glorious varieties of opinion, could also become loci of categorical crowd behavior and psychology. From Carlyle in the mid-19th century to Jacobs in the mid- and late 20th, we have visions of the city during the whole span of the Industrial Revolution. The city of the digital revolution is and could be something quite different, as the city has been changing before our eyes.

In fact, Jacobs's world has been superseded. The American Canadian architect Witold Rybczynski writes that "the most successful urban neighborhoods have attracted not the blue-collar families that she celebrated, but the rich and the young."[7] The urbanist Joel Kotkin observes that "in this new consumer city, the role that the priests and aristocrats played in imperial cities has been assumed by the global wealthy, financial engineers, media moguls, and other top business executives and service providers."[8] "The most talented, ambitious, and wealthiest people are converging as never before in a relative handful of leading superstar cities and knowledge and tech hubs," writes another prominent urbanist, Richard Florida. He calls this "the clustering force . . . of talent and economic activity" that is sorting out and re-segregating society "by income, education, and class."[9] But the segregated classes can also be in shoulder-to-shoulder proximity with each other. "Even in nouveau hipster and increasingly expensive Brooklyn," notes Kotkin, "nearly a quarter of residents—mainly African American and Latino—are below the poverty line. While the wealthy gentry shop at artisanal cheese shops and frequent trendy restaurants, one in four Brooklynites receive food stamps." Within these well-heeled and hip enclaves, Kotkin goes on, "you see the same structures, be it from Frank Gehry or some other 'starchitect.' . . . Increasingly, city skylines and waterfront developments appear remarkably similar," becoming what Dutch architect Rem Koolhaas labeled "the generic city."[10]

Jane Jacobs's vision of lively yet unpretentious sidewalks where people of different classes and opinions mix in a variety of architectural settings has been turned on its head. Within each income and professional group now there is a growing and frightening conformity, dramatized by alienating architectural sameness. Places like Manhattan, Brooklyn, and Boston are actually much better off, as their venerable past and proximity to water has engendered original aesthetics and intimate cluttering compared to many other world cities like Atlanta, São Paulo, Houston, and Los Angeles, where Jacobs's "Great Blight of Dullness" has for quite some time now been a stark reality. These differences and pathologies are crucial, since it is through their immediate surroundings that the masses, increasingly urban, experience and react to world events and geopolitics. The world just looks different, depending upon where you sit.

Nobody has described the Great Blight of Dullness better and more passionately than the late conservative English philosopher Roger Scruton. He describes the "modern vernacular composed of curtain walls or horizontal slabs, without moldings, shadows or ornaments . . . standing as a familiar adversary in our streets . . . the 'shoe box' style," he calls it, "that you can find on the edge, and increasingly in the center, of our towns. The apologists for this kind of everyday modernism," who reject the Greek and Gothic revivals, and all of the classical orders, in fact, also "reject the street as the primary public space." The result is what Scruton refers to as "the concrete wastes of a modern Western city" and the "vandalization of the landscape and townscape."[11] He implies that the postmodern city, rather than evince Jacobs's humanity, stands, at least in its architecture, as a rejection of the individual and the whole past with its traditions, in fact. And if people, on account of their surroundings, are less anchored to a past, empires, monarchies, and all the other traditions that have historically maintained states and societies are even more likely to dissolve, and to do so more quickly. Cities, therefore, in their current context, can be the conservative's worst nightmare, because classical conservatives are more interested in conserving tradition than in erecting new and uncertain ones.

And yet cities are simply where it's at. They're where politics and foreign policy get made. So it's time to investigate another, deeper layer of the urban reality that particularly concerns us, and which flows out from the somewhat dystopian visions and fears of Scruton, Kotkin, Florida, and other philosophers and urbanists.

THE FACT IS, PEOPLE, ideas, and movements are less stable in cities than in the countryside. That is because cities are where the chemistry of intellectual exchange usually happens, in surroundings if not architecturally alienating, then at least disorienting in terms of crowds and noisy factories and other types of mayhem. Marx, Lenin, Hitler, and so forth all incubated their ideas in European cities. So did Kant, Sartre, and a multitude of other philosophers. Even Mao, the son of a peasant, adopted Marxism-Leninism while at Peking University. Cities just wouldn't be cities if they weren't the places where ideas, whether good or bad, are frequently born. In fact, cities, which separate humanity from the natural world and its rhythms, as Roger Scruton's critique of their architecture demonstrates, are friendly to ideologies and to the abstractions that form them. It follows, both directly and indirectly, that chaos and crowd behavior are primarily features of cities, as those things emerge from ideas, too. History is obviously made in the countryside, a lot of it. (It was the very calmness of rural Vermont that helped enable Solzhenitsyn to gather his thoughts about the 20th century's greatest revolution.) But far more history is made in cities.

Postmodern democracies are rooted in the cosmopolitanism of city life, even as politicians constantly appeal to the rural interior. This actually is an extraordinary development. In the early and middle eras of the American republic, democracy, it could be argued, was determined by the countryside and particularly by the heartland, where a number of candidates for high office in the late 19th century (James Garfield, Benjamin Harrison, William McKinley) had all conducted successful "front porch" presidential campaigns, rarely straying far from their home districts in the Midwest, and yet ending up in the White House. Of course, elections can still be determined by voting blocs in the same heartland. But the themes and ideas of presidential campaigns now are increasingly filtered, and given their slants, through elite media establishments in cosmopolitan cities, generally on the East Coast, so that presidential elections are *national* in character in a powerful way that they never used to be. A candidate is now *packaged,* as though a product in an advertisement. *The New York Times,* which in addition to its digital website has satellite printing plants throughout the country, has a deep effect on every national and many statewide elections across the continent that would have astounded earlier generations of American politicians, even as *Times* reporters collectively represent the outlook—that is, the viewpoints and even the prejudices—of urban cosmopolitans in the global world.

That's right, prejudices, too: cosmopolitan city life can at times be intolerant and conditioned by the mood of the multitude. A lie or half-truth can ricochet endlessly within the crowd before the full truth emerges, often too late to repair reputations and affect an outcome. This is how rumors that feed anger and, in some cases, a virulent sectarian nationalism can migrate across the developing world. For here I am not just talking about the wealthy West and its cosmopolitan cities. Because of digital connectivity, cities anywhere, with their packed humanity, can be dangerous places, especially prone to information manipulation. Occasional lies, rumors, and half-truths can mar small-town life, to be sure. But the effect, the craziness, is greater in cities.

Social media and the digital-video age only amplify crowd psychology. The whole web is a city. The Trump phenomenon, which took off in vast areas of the country—urban, suburban, and rural—with its followers willing to believe just about anything, is much harder to imagine in an earlier age of technology. But *New York Times* conservative columnist Ross Douthat goes much further in describing the social media and digital world of the young, "with its pinball motion between extremes of toxic narcissism and the solidarity of the mob, its therapy-speak unmoored from real community, its conspiracism and ideological crazes."[12] This, in fact, is not necessarily an urban world, since it could afflict small-town teenagers, too. But it is more likely to be an urban or a suburban phenomenon, since here we have social media replicating the frantic conditions of the city with its numberless interactions. The mass society is upon us in a way we never imagined.

The root cause of crowd psychology is in the very spatial pattern of human contact on city streets and inside apartment blocks. Urbanity changes us. It rewires us, and as we will see, not always for the better. The new world geography is more fearsome than the old, and more destabilizing in terms of excitable public opinion. Thus will geopolitics deteriorate. This phenomenon will never be announced in the headlines. Indeed, it cannot be announced in the headlines since it is an organic process rather than an event. But you will observe it in the very heated, hysterical debates over politics, domestic and foreign, that now never cease.

The mass society was originally a creature of the late 18th and 19th centuries, as the British historian and journalist Dominic Green informs us:

"The English, American, and French Revolutions had not been aberrations; they had been harbingers of mass democracy and nationalism. The vocabulary of modern politics had arrived: constitutions, parliaments, national rights, and even natural ones. . . . Mass politics, with its parties, rallies, platforms, and voting, would become part of everyone's life. The personal would be political, and the name of the modern catechism was 'ideology.'"[13]

Ideology, with its many frightening *isms,* appeared to reach its climax in the 20th century. Aleksander Wat, a great Polish poet and intellectual whose life was coterminous with the 20th century and who had family members literally destroyed by both Nazism and Communism, wrote, in regard to Stalinism, that it was the "global answer to negation . . . that hunger for something all-embracing." There was "too much of everything. Too many people, too many ideas, too many books." This is the abundance of the city that Wat is describing. The only way to cope was with a "simple catechism," an idea that would crush all the others. Stalinism's answer was to turn the inner life "to dust." Because Stalinism killed the inner man, it represented the "exteriorization" of everything.[14]

If there were too many books and ideas and people back in Wat's day, that would be only a fraction of what one must cope with now. The soul itself, explains the contemporary Romanian philosopher Horia-Roman Patapievici, is being hollowed out because of its being bombarded by stimuli and the substitution of the inner imagination by technology: smartphones, intelligent toys, the array of electronics at malls, and artificial intelligence itself. Again, it is the city and overabundant suburbia that is the principal stage set for all of this. And within it people may be ready for a new catechism, or a succession of them.

It is the masses speaking through one voice that are the danger. Most people think that they generate their own ideas: in fact, their ideas are prepared by others who think for them. The idea that some sermon or blog post or tweet has gone viral is a sad reflection on the state of individualism.[15] Cities, as we know, have become venues for elites. And elites have an undeniable proclivity for groupthink and echo chambers, despite all their erudition. Different elite factions pick their own facts and construct opinions. The elites, even more so than the rest of us, are slaves of their smartphones. And they are always googling. And Google ranks search results in terms of how many other sites have linked to them, reinforcing such groupthink, not individuality. We speak of buzzwords and fashionable new acronyms and media feeding frenzies: these are all symptoms of urban elite groupthink. And, of course, different groupthinks collide with each other through competing silos and echo chambers.

There is just a madness about the great, pulsing cities: perhaps most negatively encapsulated by super-crowded, over-capitalized, and touristy Times Square, with crowds swerving around both the homeless and the police, whose weapons and uniforms increasingly evoke army special-forces units.

. . .

THIS BRINGS US ABRUPTLY to Oswald Spengler, the great German philosopher-historian and polymath of the early 20th century, perhaps the greatest of all time, and the author of the massive two-volume tome *The Decline of the West (Der Untergang des Abendlandes)*, published in 1918 and 1922. Spengler's vast knowledge base was a rebuke to specialization and offered an unparalleled celebration of general education. The German academy, with its emphasis on narrow credentials, despised this former schoolmaster who lived in cloistered poverty prior to his fame, and then again in isolation at the end of his life under Hitler. Although, as the decades pass, the clairvoyance of his work borders on startling, despite his difficult-to-follow discursions into the cultural nature of mathematics, the Faustian and Magian soul, the Gothic will, and so forth. The despised Spengler—he was denounced and misunderstood by nearly everyone from liberals to conservatives to the Nazis of his own time—had, in fact, studied Greek, Latin, mathematics, and the sciences, even as he had a great propensity for the arts. He has much to tell us about our time, however ultra-conservative his judgments. He saw cultural decline in everything from violent labor unrest, to sports spectacles reminiscent of the Roman Colosseum, to the emergence of the liberated "Ibsen woman," to the "whole megalopolitan literature," in fact, and to the emphasis on entertainment in just about everything. I will begin with this Spenglerian nugget: whereas the countryside produces the "folk," the "world-city," that is, in our context, the Internet, produces the "mob."[16]

Obviously, the "folk," with its connection to a mythically pure and specific homeland, and thus its innate hatred of cosmopolitanism, can be dangerous, too. Yale historian Timothy Snyder, in an early book, *The Reconstruction of Nations* (2003), connects folkishness to mass murder, as the supposed purity of a particular peasant group declares in effect the inferiority of rival and proximate groups, which in wartime conditions can then be eliminated. Both fascism and Communism have romanticized the folk and their assumed innocence and virtue. Over the decades as a foreign correspondent I can remember watching state-controlled television in a number of totalitarian states where the only entertainment on offer was the dictator's harangues interspersed with peasant dances. In such a way, the ruling chieftain governed in a folkloric paradise. In the United States, with its much higher standard of economic development and its liberal democracy, this same phenomenon is, nevertheless, apparent: obliquely, of course. In America the folk can be gun-toting, Second Amendment followers of Donald Trump and Tucker Carlson, nostalgic for an older and less complicated America, perhaps even for the Confederacy, and beset with conspiracy theories about electoral fraud, as they challenge the liberal bastions of the world media and cosmopolitan city. But the "folk" in the countryside are in demographic decline, one reason, perhaps, for their extremism in the first place, as their less complicated and more rural world of traditional values is literally eaten away by newish suburbs and exurbs and intrusive technology, as urbanization takes its toll. And as urbanization and ever more crowded suburbanization become increasingly inexorable, the future belongs to the "mob." While the folk on the political right are obsessed with conspiracy theories, the mob on the political left is obsessed with conformity: *if you don't agree with us on every point we will destroy you.*

The urban riots and looting that caused significant property damage and created pockets of anarchy in downtowns across the United States—leading to at least 200 cities announcing curfews—following the Minneapolis police murder of African American George Floyd in May 2020 were only the most extreme example of the mob in action. Gary Saul Morson, a professor of Russian literature at Northwestern University, said that those riots bore a similarity with those that preceded the Bolshevik Revolution, since in both cases you had the phenomenon of "well-intentioned liberal people," a true intelligentsia, who couldn't "bring themselves to say that lawlessness is wrong." He goes on: "When you're dragged along into something you don't really believe yourself—because otherwise you are identified with those evil people, and your primary identity is being a 'good guy'—you will wind up supporting things" that are abhorrent. "And unless there is some moral force that will stop it, the slide will accelerate."[17] In fact, both America in 2020 and Russia in 1917 demonstrated the phenomenon of genuinely liberal people socially intimidated into supporting movements to their far left, which also happened to be violent.

But the urban mob of today is rarely a physical mob. It is for our purposes a large gathering of voices all in complete agreement and bent on the destruction of a single individual, in order to intimidate the many. This kind of mob is the ultimate enemy of freedom, since its effect is to abolish individual thought itself. Remember that Nazism and Stalinism worked most often in silencing individual thought, so that everyone agreed with each other. So-called "cancel culture," in which a person's professional standing and ability to speak and publish are either reduced or, in rare cases, extinguished—as, obviously, is their ability to make a living—all on the basis of an opinion or opinions he or she may hold, is an example of such a virtual mob. This is Stalinism without any of the violence and imprisonment. Or Leninism, for that matter, since Lenin was the one who essentially invented the notion of totality, that the total result of a life is determined by one's acceptance of a single idea. If you don't believe in Communism and the rule of the party, it does not matter how good you are at your job, be it as a technician, a submariner, an engineer, or whatever, since you are nothing and must therefore be erased. I may be taking the concept of cancel culture much too far, but the similarities are eerie, and chilling.

Yet to truly imagine a more subtle and futuristic urban mob, consider the large group of *New York Times* staffers, many of them located in their apartments throughout the New York metropolitan area, in the midst of the coronavirus effective lockdown, somewhat lonely one might assume: in unison, they vented their cabin-fever frustrations on Twitter and other social media to get opinion editor James Bennet and op-ed editor James Dao removed from their jobs for running an essay by Republican senator Tom Cotton that argued in favor of using federal troops to curb the urban riots ignited by the George Floyd killing. There are two key elements in this event. One was the combination of the coronavirus restrictions *and* the riots. Were the Covid-19 restrictions not in place, *Times* staffers might have met more often in person and argued more often among themselves over coffee, and the dynamic of what transpired might have been different. It was the mid-20th-century philosopher Hannah Arendt, in *The Origins of Totalitarianism,* who suggested that repressive political systems rely on the loneliness of individuals who need to escape their condition and be part of a mass.[18] The second element in the affair was technology, which had created untold vistas for the tyranny of the 21st-century crowd, it seemed. A self-righteous mob, organized from the bottom up, had virtually defenestrated two long-standing and undeniably liberal editors at America's most influential newspaper for being insufficiently virtuous: for not being pure and therefore ideological in their opinions. As I write, the liberal mainstream media is now, two and a half years later, having second thoughts and consequently coming to Bennet's defense in a few brave instances:

Referring to an earlier article in *Semafor,* Erik Wemple, the *Washington Post* media critic, defends Bennet for saying about *New York Times* publisher A. G. Sulzberger, "He set me on fire and threw me in the garbage and used my reverence for the institution against me. This is why I was so bewildered for so long after I had what felt like all my colleagues treating me like an incompetent fascist." In fact, as Wemple documents, Sulzberger, who initially supported Bennet for running a legitimate opinion by Senator Cotton, a potential presidential candidate at the time, quickly folded upon the onslaught from the mob at *The New York Times,* members of which tweeted that the very publication of Cotton's essay "puts Black . . . staff in danger," without explaining how that was possible. Sulzberger and other *Times* officials ran the Cotton essay through a rigorous second fact-checking process, even though the piece had already been rigorously fact-checked, in the hope of discrediting it. And this was all because of a social-media mob of generally younger staff. As it happened, the second fact-checking substantiated the first. Wemple called attention to the "hollowness" of the entire internal uproar at the *Times,* even as he confessed for reasons of "cowardice and midcareer risk management" his own two-and-a-half-year delay in writing this.[19] Jonathan Chait, a pundit and writer for *New York* magazine, believes that Wemple is not alone in his view of how he and others spinelessly accepted Bennet's and Dao's defenestration in the moment that it happened. "It is an unhealthy culture that forces people to suppress their doubts and mouth platitudes for fear of losing their livelihoods," Chait writes, adding that "what Wemple's confession reveals is that these purges have a multiplier effect: For every person humiliated or fired for a small or nonexistent offense, many other people will refuse to criticize even transparently absurd left-wing pieties."[20]

Another example of such a piety was the unwillingness to tolerate even the idea that the coronavirus might have originated in a laboratory in China. This effectively silenced the media on the subject—until such a possibility was revealed as indeed plausible. There are few things more destabilizing for geopolitics than for the media in each competing country to give the masses a distorted version of reality on account of groupthink and the fear of facing an unpleasant truth. This is how governments can be influenced by the mob, and, on occasion, drift into unnecessary wars.

Spengler, in *The Decline of the West,* saw all of this coming, after a fashion. For it was journalists and their profession that may have terrified him the most.

"As for the modern press," Spengler writes, "the sentimentalist may beam with contentment when it is constitutionally 'free'—but the realist merely asks at whose disposal it is.... No tamer has his animals more under his power" than the press, he goes on. "Unleash the people as reader-mass and it will storm through the streets and hurl itself upon the target indicated.... The Press today is an army ... with journalists as officers, and readers as soldiers.... A more appalling caricature of freedom of thought cannot be imagined. Formerly a man did not dare to think freely. Now he dares, but cannot; his will to think is only a willingness to think to order, and this is what he feels as *his* liberty."[21]

Spengler died in 1936, before the utter destruction of World War II would give additional breadth to his gloomy vision of civilizational decline, and before European postwar reconstruction, with its popular arts, cinema glamour, and prosperity, would, in more subtle ways, verify his observations. Actually, Spengler's words about the press would provide a vivid account of how Julius Streicher's virulently anti-Semitic newspaper *Der Sturmer* played a central role in stirring up Nazi mobs against the Jews in the late 1930s and beyond. And Spengler's fears about the media still have resonance in America today, however more nuanced and less lethal have become the examples of this.

Who can deny, for example, the sheer cultural and political power of *The New York Times*? Or Fox News, for that matter? No senator's speech or revelatory book even has the ability to move the needle on public opinion like a well-placed story, purportedly about news, but in fact barely masking an opinion, appearing on *The New York Times* home page or in prime time on Fox. Of course, the *Times* is professional in just so many ways that Fox is not, making it ultimately less lethal. Nevertheless, their points of view in both cases have drifted away from the strict middle ground in the aftermath of the print-and-typewriter age.

In fact, the press, or the media I should say, is more powerful now than ever in history because of the vividness of words and images as they flash on smartphones or computer screens in the digital-video age: an age which incorporates the Hollywood mindset of manipulating reality in order to distort how we think about the great issues of the day—replete with rumors, exaggerations, and character assassination. For it is impossible to imagine our present political polarization except in the age of Internet news, which drives people to sites of extreme opinions that validate their preexisting prejudices, turning them into mobs.[22]

And digital-video technology, precisely because it is given to manipulation, is inherently controlling. Think of how the great film directors of the 20th century were able to take over your mind for a few hours: a new experience for audiences that previous generations had never known. Theater may be as old as the ancient

Greeks, but, once again, it has been the new technology that has amplified the force of the theatrical experience.[23] Spengler intuited this with his fear of the media and what it could potentially become. Combine the urban horde that Spengler so well described with the mass media of today and the results can be frightening.

All of this applies not only to the United States but to countries throughout the world, where public opinion regularly becomes inflamed on account of the new media technology. Such inflammation can have its positive effect, sure, as when the deployment of social media challenges dictatorships: Chinese citizens protesting extreme Covid restrictions, or Iranian citizens protesting the mandatory use of the hijab. Yet the mob principle still holds. Some mobs will do good, it goes without saying. But the future will naturally be one of different kinds of mobs, forming and re-forming, owing to technology and urbanization, since most of us already live in cities and crowded suburbs, and this will be more so in the decades to come, as people in the developing world will increasingly live in slum encampments on the outskirts of cities, yet connected to the world through their devices. And that will create an altered dynamic to history. Observe the surge of public hysteria, expressed through social media, that occurs in cities throughout India and Pakistan whenever geopolitical tensions rise in the nuclear-armed Asian subcontinent. The point is to see social media and digital-video technology not in isolation, but in combination with other geopolitical forces, such as urbanization and weaponry. Unlike thermonuclear warheads, the new weaponry—hypersonic missiles, precision-guided bombs, small-scale tactical nuclear weapons—are designed to be actually used. Consider the mix of such munitions controlled by governments that are besieged by their own social-media-enraged populations: not only in democracies, but also in dictatorships, where the very lack of political freedom can make people at key moments even more prone to rebellion. This is where it gets scary, making Spengler's passages resonate.

SPENGLER'S BROAD CONCEPT OF civilizational decline, linked to the influence of the media but not exclusively to it, is akin to that of the medieval Arab scholar Abd al-Rahman Ibn Khaldun's own famous theory, expressed in the latter's *Muqaddimah: An Introduction to History*. Ibn Khaldun, born in 1332, was a writer, thinker, traveler, and historian of the caliber of the Italian Renaissance, though he lived in North Africa. He advised sultans and ministers not only in his native Tunis but also in the courts of Moorish Spain and the Maghreb, as Morocco was then known. His great idea about history begins with the Bedouin, with whom he was so familiar, since the desert "is the basis and reservoir of civilization and cities." This is true because before there can be luxury and opulence there must be the bare necessities, which the Bedouin restrict themselves to, until, over time, they become strong enough to become sedentary themselves and infiltrate cities and towns, or start them on their own. Ibn Khaldun observed that whereas the Bedouin aspired to sedentary life in the town, the townspeople had no such aspiration regarding life in the wilderness. Thus, the pattern of history was established in his mind. It is one of nomads gradually moving into the towns and thus building dynasties of their own, until they, too, become wealthy and soft in their ways and are overtaken by new and different nomads. This is, broadly speaking, how dynasties decay, as they "have a natural life span like individuals." Luxury leads to strength initially, with its arts and money and power, but then decadence sets in, and the provincials, sensing weakness, attack the basis of city life and its morals.[24]

Thus, before there was a Spengler there was an Ibn Khaldun.

As Spengler explains it, any large group operates as an "organism," which is born, grows old, and dies. The highest form of group achievement constitutes "civilization," which represents the "fulfilment and finale of a culture," before it deteriorates and crumbles.[25] That is, cultures become increasingly wealthy and sophisticated over the decades and centuries, producing great works of art and learning, and in the process become themselves decadent and therefore weak, and are then overtaken by other cultures (or by Bedouin tribes assaulting the city, in Ibn Khaldun's rendering). These nomads, arguably akin to Spengler's "folk," who assault the centers of civilization, are particularly aggressive and sure of themselves, and in the long story of their subsequent growth and cultural development they repeat the cycle, as they, too, become *civilized*.

There is a vague allegory here with the red states assaulting the blue ones. But people from rural Kansas and such are not moving to New York and taking over with their conservative values. That's not what's really implied for our own age in Spengler and Ibn Khaldun. Indeed, it has been quite common for many decades now for artists and writers from the interior of America or other conservative quarters to move to places like New York, live out their lives there, and adopt wholeheartedly the values of a cosmopolitan worldview. Andy Warhol from Pittsburgh, William Styron from various places in the South, and Calvin Trillin from Kansas City are just a few of a plethora of examples of artists who came to the Big City and changed accordingly, or became their true, inner selves. Because America is a democratic union, the assault from the less culturally sophisticated, conservative quarters on the cosmopolitan bastions like New York is occurring in the realm of national politics only, through the media. Thus, in a political sense, the countryside is assailing the city, which has grown effete in the course of many decades of luxury and cultural refinement.

Who will win this epic battle that has been building for several election cycles? I don't know. But I do know that the drama is principally playing out in—and being interpreted by—a cosmopolitan media located in the great cities. It is all about the cities, in fact: what they have become, and the negative reaction to them in what F. Scott Fitzgerald famously called "that vast obscurity . . . where the dark fields of the republic rolled on under the night."[26]

FOR SPENGLER THE CITY is the world, where *the decline of the West* is indeed happening before one's eyes. The city with its media was the stage set for Spengler's entire theory, and more vaguely Ibn Khaldun's for that matter, and for the growth, maturation, decadence, and decline of many a culture: since Spengler clearly sees the city, and each upscale mall when you get right down to it, as representing both the apex and downfall of Man.

I witnessed this most intensely in the Communist expanse of Central and Eastern Europe and the former Soviet Union in the 1980s and post-Communist 1990s, where the cities were vibrant and the rural hinterlands were zones of alcoholism, near-chaos, and brutal underdevelopment, so that these places weren't countries so much as city-states, separated from each other by limitless zones of darkness, in which fabulous wealth accumulated within a radius of a few square miles in a short-lived era of Klondike capitalism, before the effect of European Union membership began to stabilize and even out development in Central and Eastern Europe. Russia, of course, is still afflicted by this extreme version of Spengler's vision. One of the many reasons the West is the West is that its rural hinterlands, increasingly encroached upon by suburbs and exurbs, are nice places to live, where roads, schools, and hospitals are decent, even if the culture lacks the sophistication of the metropole; and even though the towns inhabit the nation-state, while the cities inhabit world civilization. It is the very development of infrastructure in the rural precincts of the West that allows for its glamorous cities in the first place: outside the West, where people flee en masse their underdeveloped hinterlands without economic opportunities, cities are both fringed and compromised, with vast slums and shantytowns, which function as way stations for the rural migrants as they fight for employment in the cities. One reason why there are more and more mega-cities is because of this uneven development. Spengler doesn't discuss any of this because he died in 1936, long before the rise and fall of Communism in Central and Eastern Europe, and before globalization, whose bad side effects have included new shantytowns with relatively poor infrastructure of electricity and potable water across the developing world, especially in Latin America and sub-Saharan Africa. Yet all of this actually works to intensify Spengler's strategic emphasis on the world-city and its pathologies. For the world-city, with its access to the Internet, whether in a luxury high-rise or a slum, is a place of global culture and the intense yearning for more of it that undermine the nation-state.

Inside the world-city, as we know, is the "press," as Spengler calls it, which embodies, in turn, the tip of the spear in terms of civilizational decline of which the city is the heart. Here is where urbanity and the original liberal hopes associated with it—especially those of Jane Jacobs—begin to turn in upon themselves, as the press, by leading the masses by the neck in terms of political and cultural values, becomes the foremost incubator of the mob, even as the "folk" rebel against it. *Style,* which the elite newspapers and other periodicals are ultimately all about, especially in their glossy magazine sections that often go under the very name, is ultimately the enemy of civilization and the agent of its eventual demise. This is because, in both Spengler's and Ibn Khaldun's interpretation, *style* indicates the ultimate refinement of the body, with all its clothes and jewelry and perfume, where appearances are everything and substance consequently nothing. This, of course, leads to the worship of youth over age, despite the acquired wisdom of the latter, since youth is by biological definition physically beautiful and age consequently not so. Such is the height of civilization, and the beginning of its drawn-out regression, Spengler and Ibn Khaldun suggest.

The triumph of youth over age, rather than leading to hope, as conventional wisdom has it, leads instead to disintegration. Of course, in demographic terms we are an aging society, but in culture and media terms the emphasis is increasingly on youth. I remember a *New York Times* reporter showing me a memo he had received from a top editor, exhorting his subordinates to appeal in every story and review to new young readers. The top editor appeared unaware of how age carries the memories of a culture with all of its traditions, in which youth has first to be instructed. To put youth on an even higher pedestal, therefore, is to destroy civilization. And yet that is what the news and advertising media do.

Spengler was a dark and moody German conservative, and thus he is not an altogether objective interpreter. Remember, however, that as the philosopher Roger Scruton has observed, conservatism is about home and hearth and tradition as an anchor in society, to save us all from becoming "atomic individuals, disinfected of the past, and living like ants within their metallic and functional shells," a reference to the traditionless modern architecture—so central to the city of the 21st century—that Scruton hates so much and cannot escape from, because it is just *there,* unavoidable.[27]

Spengler and Scruton both, as well as Solzhenitsyn, who hated the worship of youth and felt that the downfall of the Russian royal family, whatever its iniquities, meant the loss of tradition that led inevitably to the Bolshevik nightmare, all worry that the pillars of civilization are being pulled down by modernism and postmodernism, with chaos and fragmentation in their wake. Remember that Solzhenitsyn was like Pope John Paul II in that both were as critical of the West as of their own Communist societies.

SPENGLER SAYS THAT WITHOUT traditions, which ultimately are rooted in the soil, a nation or civilization loses "form."[28] The most obvious sign of an advanced civilization losing "form" is its takeover by the *money culture* in the cities, which has little sense of a past and where it came from, and little concern either.[29] The money culture of bankers, stockbrokers, real estate entrepreneurs, media moguls, and their like goes hand in hand with the overseas adventures of imperialism, which together signify the end of the West. While empire in historical terms may have been politically stabilizing—the fall of the Hohenzollern and Habsburg empires gave us Hitler—the process of accumulating imperial possessions leads to decadence and decline, according to Spengler. This is because extreme concentrations of wealth in the cities can be a sign of extraordinary state power, which, in turn, tempts nations and states to go abroad both to extend that power and to protect their interests, which, by virtue of the very existence of their money cultures, are now international.

Washington think tanks, too, are part of the money culture, as their operating funds come from corporate donations as well as from extremely wealthy individuals. And lo and behold, such think tanks often advocate military adventures abroad, in one form or another, just and unjust; it makes no difference for our purposes, since imperialism is often implicit rather than explicit. To wit, the word *imperialism* is disparaged in the United States, even as America has been in an imperial-like situation since 1945. All this isn't true just of New York and Washington but also of medieval Venice, the early-modern Netherlands, and many other empires made up of bankers, adventurers, and all manner of slick operators. The civilization in question has triumphed, in other words, and there is often nowhere to go but down, as its power brokers, who in America's case come from all over the world, as immigrants and ambitious passport-seekers, have only a vague sense of a past that originated with sod-busters deep inside the American continent in the course of the 19th century. The continuity has been lost. That is why imperialism is both the height and the end of the line of great civilizations. Indeed, nobody can deny that the American empire from the close of World War II to the early 21st century has been grand, in terms of preserving a semblance of world order. But as America's relative share of global wealth has gradually declined, and the world as I've described it has become increasingly unmanageable, we may well be on a downward trajectory.

For this is the heart of Spengler's story (even if he rarely discusses America). Spengler would look at skyrocketing Manhattan property values over the course of the decades, military adventures in Afghanistan and Iraq, and Pentagon arms buildups against China and Russia, and yawn, for he had seen it all before in his voluminous studies of wars and civilizations spanning the millennia. This does not mean that America is wrong to rise to the challenge of a more aggressive China and Russia; only that it contributes to a larger historical effect that can be tragic for America.

Spengler, through it all, is the ultimate generalist, seeing history from a godlike height and span, mixing and matching historical periods of empires and dynasties across the globe, talking about the "Gothic" period of China, the "Merovingian" period of Babylon, and so forth. His perspective has perhaps never been equaled. That is because his education, by choice, was horizontal rather than vertical. He studied a vast variety of subjects in history, science, geography, and culture, literally without the time to pursue any one of them toward the type of advanced degree qualifying him in the eyes of his peers as an *expert*. We often talk about the benefits of a liberal arts education; well, Spengler gave himself the monumental version of one. He might well have looked down on the liberal arts in American colleges, even in their glory days of the post–World War II era, as still too narrow. Now, obviously, we have gone over to the other extreme, where we inhabit a world populated by specialists with exceedingly stove-piped visions of reality, who are therefore apt to have poorer judgment than the widely read Spengler. And this poorer judgment, multiplied across the population—especially among the elites—makes for an innumerable debris of bad decisions subtly weakening our civilization, and there is little any of us can do about it, because we can't put our finger exactly on it. After all, as knowledge accumulates in so many fields, expertise provides the only way forward. We simply cannot avoid it. And yet a regime of experts risks constituting an indefinable darkness, since experts can periodically be wrong and themselves subject to groupthink. That's why, as messy and unsatisfying as politics can be, there is no escape from being governed by politicians rather than by experts.

Spengler goes on with his thesis of civilizational decline. He writes that the "gleaming autumn of style" signifies a culture just before it begins its long death throes, since an obsession with refined taste, as we've said, is the beginning of decadence. And the arts, it also goes without saying, are "urban" and "therefore secular," because true religious belief is absent in the great *world-cities,* which have insufficient "soil ties." Spengler writes rapturously: "Dresden and Vienna are the homes of this late and soon-extinguished fairyland of *visible* chamber music, of curved furniture and mirror-halls, and . . . porcelain. It is the last supreme expression, lit by an autumnal sun, of the Western soul." Notice: everything that succeeds early- and mid-19th-century chamber music—be it the impressionism of great composers like Debussy and Saint-Saëns, the breakthrough modernism of Stravinsky, or the Great American Songbook epitomized by Rodgers and Hammerstein and Stephen Sondheim—denotes a cultural decline, however stirring; however beautiful, moving, and innovative it may be. Even such a classic as *West Side Story,* with lyrics by Sondheim and music by Leonard Bernstein, which broke the boundaries of popular music, and came at the height of the American Century and American power—much as Sophocles's searing tragedy *Oedipus Rex* came at the height of Athenian power—probably would not have impressed Spengler, as it would still have signified a regression from the likes of Franz Schubert and Ludwig van Beethoven. For Spengler's context is nothing less than the vast historical and cultural flows of centuries and millennia. Thus, to continue the point, such a classic American musical as *Oklahoma!,* which helped rally the home front during World War II, is, alas, something crude and simplistic compared to the delicate movements of Robert Schumann and Felix Mendelssohn. Spengler is not crazy, much as we'd like to think so; it is just that his perspective is so long as to be inhuman.

As for painting, anything after the likes of Manet and Cezanne "is impotence and falsehood," at least in Spengler's view. In 1918, Spengler actually wrote that "every single art-school could be shut down without art being affected in the slightest." Nothing, therefore, punctuates the centuries-long decline of the West like modern art, because, among other things—and like the climax of civilization itself—modern art is tied to the abstractions of the city and despises any link to the land. And whatever "disconnects itself from the land becomes rigid" and, in the final analysis, ideological. The late journalist and novelist Tom Wolfe comprehended some of this in his book *The Painted Word* (1975). Wolfe wrote that painting in the course of the 20th century had become not a visual experience but a visual illustration of theories of art propounded by a select group of critics. In fact, he wrote, the art world had become dominated by a narrow and limited, über-urban group of wealthy collectors, museums located in superstar cities, and a handful of influential critics, who together determined what people saw in galleries and museums. Modern art was also something else: it was about Freudian introspection, decomposition, and African as well as American, and Asian as well as European forms. And that, of course, can be liberating. But because it owed little to geographical limits, and thus even less to American and European landscapes, it had freed itself from the "deep soil ties" that Spengler extols.[30]

On one crucial level, Spengler is wrong. One of the greatest museums I have ever visited is Peggy Guggenheim's collection of modern art located on the Grand Canal in Venice, which displays the works of Pablo Picasso, Constantin Brâncuși, Max Ernst, Paul Klee, Wassily Kandinsky, Andy Warhol, and more. What Spengler obviously misses is that there is a progression beyond European art and culture that is not necessarily decadent. This progression, by being abstract, and by encompassing other traditions, manifests a direction toward a universal aesthetic that is, in turn, evidence of a smaller and more connected world. And that world, precisely by being smaller and connected, is inherently tumultuous and unstable. So Spengler, even as he is a reactionary in terms of art and culture, contributes to my point about geopolitics.

THE SOIL TIES THAT Spengler extols were lost with the Machine Age before his book appeared. Witness Igor Stravinsky's ballet and orchestral concert *The Rite of Spring,* first heard and performed in Paris in 1913, on the eve of World War I, though virtually nobody foresaw war at the time. The music was "jarring. It lacked ornamentation, moral intimation, and even, for the most part, melody," writes the Latvian-born Canadian historian and cultural critic Modris Eksteins. There was a brutality about the music, he goes on. "If there was any hope, it was in the energy and fertility of life, not in morality."[31] The audience was shocked by the music, which, as T. S. Eliot put it, seemed to "transform the rhythm of the steppes into the scream of the motor horn, the rattle of machinery, the grind of wheels, the beating of iron and steel, the roar of the underground railway, and the other barbaric cries of modern life."[32]

Like Stravinsky, Eliot may actually have been more hopeful than Spengler. Spengler is without any uplifting beauty, unlike Eliot. But Eliot was also fearful of the future. In 1913, when Stravinsky's *Rite of Spring* was first performed, Eliot was just starting to burst forth as a writer. In time, with his grand allusions to technology and historical fate, he would tower above virtually the entire canon of American and British poetry in the 20th century, so much of which was strictly confessional and introverted, with the spellbinding interiority of Robert Frost's landscape poetry being the great exception. Eliot, by helping to invent poetic modernism, saw through the transparencies of the modern world to its message of alienation underneath. To Eliot, the modern world was an "immense panorama of futility and anarchy," a pile of fragments.[33] Whereas the Austrian Rainer Maria Rilke, a near-contemporary of Eliot, whose own work with its dizzying introspection spanned the borders of Europe and escaped geography, embodied the poetic miracle which rose above the masses, it was Eliot the poetic realist who dealt with the effect of war and history upon the masses.[34]

Eliot's poem *The Waste Land,* published in 1922, the same year as Spengler's second volume of *The Decline of the West,* was famously all about the "breakdown of forms"; the intermingling of epochs, languages, and traditions and the destruction of unitary cultures that had been rooted in the soil.[35] The poem, written in the aftermath of one world war and before another, ends with an "apocalypse," and yet its "discontinuities . . . feel like home," according to the contemporary critic James Parker, on account of the crises of the world today at the geopolitical level and postmodern life at the micro-level.[36]

The Waste Land is a poem that begins with a vision of idyllic aristocratic life in Europe that is wiped out by World War I, leaving only a dead imprint of "stony rubbish" in its wake, a "heap of broken images," and ends after a kaleidoscopic tour of mystifying symbols, with the repetition of a Sanskrit word, *shantih,* that implies "the peace that passeth all understanding." In between are five sections—"The Burial of the Dead," "A Game of Chess," "The Fire Sermon," "Death by Water," and "What the Thunder Said"—that are themselves laden with obscure literary and classical analogies: a tarot reading, a walk through London as if through a city of the dead, the absence of water and only dry rock in the landscape, and "hooded hordes swarming." He writes, "A crowd flowed under London Bridge, so many / I had not thought death had undone so many." It is almost impossible for the layman to understand exactly what is going on in the poem, and critics have argued about its line-by-line meaning for a century now. The poem works, though. It reads like a sweaty, nightmarish dream forgotten instantly upon waking. And yet the abstract horror of it endures and has been integrated almost into the popular culture on account of its underlying power, which, in turn, relies on its uncanny echo of our own disjointed, anarchy-bordering crises: political, cultural, and psychological. As the narrator says near the end, before reciting the Sanskrit incantation, "These fragments I have shored against my ruins."[37]

Not only in *The Waste Land,* but in his earlier breakthrough poems, "The Love Song of J. Alfred Prufrock" and "Gerontion," Eliot employs the thematic backdrop of vast, bleak, cosmopolitan, and alienating "Unreal" cities to describe the modern dilemma, and to expose the postmodern one, too.[38] The mid-20th-century American poet Delmore Schwartz writes that "modern life may be compared to a foreign country in which a foreign language is spoken," incomprehensible to us, but not to Eliot, who has described this new world where, as Schwartz intimates, national culture has been eradicated but international culture is still too superficial to take its place, as occurs in the world's great cities today. This is the Waste Land.[39]

Eliot and Spengler were contemporaries, and though one was a poet and the other a philosopher-historian, they were really talking about the same thing: the decline and breakdown of traditional civilizations based on language and geography.

Post–World War I literary modernism, as exemplified by Eliot and his editor for *The Waste Land,* Ezra Pound, was really only the first stage of literature coming to grips with breakdown and collapse. The second stage came after World War II, famously with the existentialist French writers Jean-Paul Sartre and Albert Camus. Existentialism was a response to the "emergency" of daily life in the modern world, expressed through a precise detailing of one's thoughts on paper, page after page, wrote the poet and critic Hayden Carruth. Reality, according to the existentialists, can only be what one individual "knows and experiences."[40] Thus, a crowd, or mob, or folk is by definition untruth. Whereas Eliot's poetry was about panoramic political and cultural failure, French existentialism was about the neurosis of personal life: it constituted a drilling-down from civilization and culture to the level of the singular human being. It was, in part, a response to the Holocaust and the wider devastation of World War II, which had worked to erase the individual altogether. Indeed, in their fiction both Sartre and Camus are able to explain the most abstract of concepts through the lives of average, even pathetic, individuals. Like few other writers save for James Joyce and Henry James, for example, Sartre and Camus capture human consciousness and stream-of-thought, even those of criminals. That is why their fiction is so central to their philosophy. They were intellectuals who nevertheless understood common people and their problems, however radical and unrealistic Sartre's own far-left politics may have been.

Finally, we have the post–Cold War era mixed with the age of digital and cyber technology, which began in 1989 and really gathered steam in the early 21st century. Because of the way that the cyber and digital age both enrich and intensify individual experience and consciousness, and because of a new technological ability for individuals to network with each other below the threshold of political authority—so that they can challenge prevailing power structures—the current age demonstrates an obsession with self, evinced by anxiety on one hand and identity politics on the other. From Eliot's civilizational breakdown to Sartre's breakdowns of neurotic individuals, mixed with the discovery of individual agency, we now have the chaos of anxiety-ridden individuals, again, obsessed with self, coming together in new crowd formations. The spectacle at *The New York Times* where a digital mob sought to end the career of two eminently experienced and liberal editors had been, in cultural and civilizational terms, decades in the making. So too might be the throngs of elite college students gathering together in packed encampments to, in effect, support Hamas, despite its October 7, 2023, atrocity against Jews.

CONSIDER ALL OF THE above in light of the human geography of the 21st century: vast, technologically connected metroplexes, cities and suburbs both, particularly but not exclusively in the West, with their own adjacent hinterlands for weekend retreats, where religion has been replaced by exercise and consumerism. Jane Jacobs's liberal vision of the vibrant sidewalk of different classes fights for survival, while the conservative Roger Scruton is appalled about humans "living like ants within their metallic and functional shells." Forget about wide-open spaces. They will exist mainly for tourism. By 2050, virtually the entire population of Arizona will live in the Greater Tucson–Phoenix urban-suburban corridor. The United States as a whole is overwhelmingly urban, with 83 percent of its population now living in cities and their immediate environs. In China, 65 percent of the population is urban; in Russia, 75 percent. These figures will go on rising.

The urbanist Richard Florida writes:

"Over the next century or two, the world's urban population is projected to almost triple, peaking at 85 percent of a total global population of between 11 and 12 billion. As many as 8.6 billion of those urbanites will live in the cities of the developing world (many of which have yet to be built), while just 1.2 billion or so will occupy the cities of the advanced nations."[41] (Though his figures are too high, as world population will peak below 11 billion, his larger point is accurate.)

In sub-Saharan Africa, 85 percent of the population will eventually live in the cities in a number of countries. The bush, or forest, or savanna will only partially define Africa. Much of the political drama will play out in the slums and shantytowns occupied by the ruralized urban poor—not just in Africa, but in the Asian subcontinent and Latin America, too: migrants from the countryside, who, despite the superficially ugly and overcrowded conditions, with dwellings of sheet iron and breeze block all jumbled together, will still believe there is more economic opportunity close to the capital or big city. This was the world I introduced readers to in "The Coming Anarchy" over three decades ago. It is a world of intense human striving, of self-help organizations, committees, petitioners—for these are the ambitious ones, who have deserted the dead-end existences of the far-flung villages plagued by militias and other lawless bands. Yet the conditions in these shantytowns can be really bad: uncertain electricity, uncertain plumbing, dirty water, bad air, and the plague of sheer overcrowding. Then there are the youth gangs, shakedown artists, and other such who exist by virtue of the absence or insufficiency of proper police. These places can be waste lands in a different sense than in the high-end conurbations of the West and developed world. I say "can be," because it all depends on the human interactions and what encourages them: if the degree of aggression and intimidation is reasonably low, and opportunities exist for enough of the inhabitants, such shantytowns can be way stations to the working and middle classes, as I observed in Turkish slums in the 1990s.

What unites African slums with the tony cities and suburbs of the West is the perennial struggle to avoid the intimidating pressures of groupthink and giving in to the bullies—physical or intellectual—while at the same time retaining the ability to work together for social and economic betterment. Whether a young tough demands a bribe or an editor or digital mob demands conformist language from you in order for you to keep your job, it may amount to a similar level of evil.

The cities, because of their crowded conditions, are an intensification of existence and therefore of politics. Even if you don't buy Spengler's argument, or Malthus's, or buy only parts of them, and find only parts of them relevant, they should at least make you nervous given the demographics of the 21st century. Nobody will declare his or her views as driven by ideological abstraction and crowd psychology because he or she happens to live in a teeming urban setting or an architecturally and socially conformist suburban one. But it will be there, just below the surface, having its effect, multiplied by billions. It is a conceit of the modern world, to repeat Solzhenitsyn, that history is governed by reason.

The French Revolution, the Russian Revolution, Kristallnacht, Maoist China's Cultural Revolution, and the Iranian Revolution are some examples of the madness of urban crowds coupled with the irresistibility of extremism that helped to give early-modern and modern history their horrifying direction. Even in the United States, urban riots, which can be motivated by a demand for racial justice, contain a violent edge that has, in turn, for better and sometimes for worse, dramatically affected the course of domestic politics. Urban riots are almost always a common element in regime crises, and not only in the developing world with ever larger cities. The 21st century, in other words, will be increasingly tumultuous. Indeed, the heart of dictatorship is to prevent the formation of spontaneous crowds, which can form more easily than ever before because of social-media technology. "The crowd!" Solzhenitsyn writes. "A strange special being, both human and inhuman . . . where each individual was released from his usual responsibility and was multiplied in strength."[42] The psychology of the crowd, or mob, is thus: "Show us who [next] to tear to pieces."[43]

THOUGH TECHNOLOGY HAS KEPT evolving, the roots of the permanent crisis in the 21st century continue to lie in what went wrong in the 20th. Nazism and Communism shared two decisive elements: the safety of the crowd and the yearning for purity. I remember being in Bucharest, Romania, in November 1981, observing immense crowds of people, marching in the freezing cold, shouting, "*Ceaușescu, pace, Ceaușescu, pace*" (Ceaușescu, peace, Ceaușescu, peace). They were demanding peace and nuclear disarmament, while also celebrating the totalitarian dictator. Moral purity and blind obedience were the messages of the crowd. Sacred tradition, which "cannot be contrived or learned," according to the great British translator of Russian literature Max Hayward, had been utterly destroyed by the Stalinist dictator of Romania, and in its place was socialist "progress," like the "mechanical movement of a clock hand," proclaiming that the future has only one direction.[44] Such mindless crowds cast off all humanizing and historical tradition, including religion, and thus give themselves up to ideology in one form or another. They do this by destroying the memory and existence of the individual: who, being an individual, may deviate from the political direction demanded by the crowd.

In *Crowds and Power,* first published in German in 1960, the Bulgarian Jewish philosopher Elias Canetti may have written the most intuitive book about the crisis of the West over the past hundred years. Spengler's tome argues that Western civilization, like all civilizations, is ultimately ephemeral and tied to the development of the city. Canetti's book explains the actual mechanics of this decline. Canetti, like Hannah Arendt, wrote in the immediate wake of the ravages of Nazism and Stalinism and had an especial knack about the present and future. Canetti won the Nobel Prize in Literature mainly for this book, which I first read in paperback in Stalinist Romania, where I encountered some of the very sorts of crowds Canetti wrote about. He and Arendt both understood that the worst tyrannies had their origins in the isolation and loneliness of the individual, which leads to the most fearsome crowd formations. That is, as we shall see, the mob is made up of lonely people.

Canetti's early work of fiction, *Auto-da-Fé,* lays the groundwork for *Crowds and Power* by dissecting the neurosis of a man who lives alone, entirely for his library, since for him books have replaced human beings. He has minimal contact with others and is tormented by his housekeeper: "You draw closer to the truth by shutting yourself off from mankind. . . . The greatest danger which threatens a man of learning is to lose himself in talk. . . . He panted for silence as others do for air."[45] This, of course, is the profile of a man who prefers to be alone. After all, he is mentally enriched by his books and learning. But the vast majority of people want to escape their loneliness and be one with others. Canetti, who has explored loneliness in all its aspects, and from all directions, is best prepared to explore the phenomenon of the crowd.

The crowd, Canetti writes, emerges from the need of the lonely individual to conform with others. He wants to lose himself and escape from his isolation by literally rubbing shoulders with others, and feeling the breath of others upon his neck. It is only within the crowd that he can escape the innate human "fear of being touched" by a stranger. Because he can't exert dominance on his own, he exerts it through a crowd that speaks with one voice. He was nothing before the creation of this crowd and now he is everything. The crowd's urge is always to grow, rescuing others from their loneliness, and consuming all hierarchies, since the goal of a lonely individual is always to be noticed and to dominate his betters. "*Within the crowd there is equality,*" Canetti emphasizes.[46] Yet the crowd feels persecuted and demands retribution, because lonely individuals are always bitter about something. Thus, the crowd sees itself as entirely pure, having attained the highest virtue. After all, the lonely individual, in his own thoughts at least, can do no wrong. And he receives justification of this inside the crowd, where for the first time he feels he has power. This is how tyranny begins.

A principal aim of the crowd is to hunt down the insufficiently virtuous, like those *on the wrong side of history,* because, after all, to pronounce someone as such is to presume to know the direction of history, a category of knowledge not given to anyone. For even those who fight against the most abject despotisms can't be sure how events will turn out. All they can do is struggle. To claim categorically to know the future, therefore, falls within the realm of ideology, of which the crowd, or mob, is a principal weapon.

Canetti as a writer is as relentless and obsessive as the crowds he describes, breaking them down and cataloging them over the course of more than 500 pages. The original "crowd crystal," he writes, was "the *pack,*" a small horde or band of "ten or twenty men," engaged often in hunting, which in prehistory was the "universal expression of communal excitement." Derivative of the "hunting pack" is the "baiting crowd." The victim here is "known and clearly marked." The victim is also near, and the crowd won't rest or disband until the victim is killed or punished in some way. The existence of the baiting crowd leads to the phenomenon of public executions, which are connected to the practice of collective killing. "The real executioner is the crowd gathered round the scaffold," Canetti writes. The most primitive of all crowd packs engaged in collective killing is the lynch mob, which thinks itself human only because its members do not actually sink their teeth into the victim. The victim here looks different from the crowd. He is clearly not one of them. And the fact that he runs away increases the blood lust of the crowd when its members find him. Thus does racism in the American South have the most primitive roots. Even inflation, Canetti declares, is a "crowd phenomenon," since as the unit of money loses its value and identity, the individuals who own it feel depreciated, and as they cannot admit their own depreciation to themselves, a crowd comes into being that finds a victim for such depreciation, a scapegoat. The inflation in Germany that helped bring Hitler to power was one of the most extreme in economic history. And the victim that the crowd chose for vengeance was the Jews, who were seen to be "on good terms with money when others did not know how to manage it," and thus were a natural target for the crowd to shift all the blame onto. Canetti, throughout this book, is essentially explaining many of the worst evils of history—and how they could come about—through the phenomenon of crowds. But he also writes about many kinds of crowds that are not evil, such as "reversal crowds." He explains that "revolutions are times of reversal; those who have been defenseless for so long suddenly find teeth." Depending upon the circumstances, this can be either good or bad. Again, the crowd, in Canetti's eyes, helps form the bedrock of the human experience, with an especial emphasis on the dark side.[47]

The tyranny of the crowd has many other aspects, but Canetti says its most blatant and riveting form is that of the "questioner," that is, of the accuser. "When used as an intrusion of power," the accusing crowd "is like a knife cutting into the flesh of the victim. The questioner knows what there is to find, but he wants actually to touch it and bring it to light." Naturally, the more hostile the questions, the greater the delight of the crowd.[48] Congressional hearings on both sides of the political divide have over the years and decades become an increasingly vivid example of this, rising to the level of spectacle. Though perhaps the greatest spectacle of absolute madness abetted by crowd psychology occurred in the late 1940s and 1950s when Congress, under the baleful influence of Wisconsin Republican senator Joseph McCarthy, orchestrated a witch hunt against U.S. diplomats and other area specialists, who it accused of leading a Communist conspiracy that resulted in the "loss" of China to Mao Zedong's forces. Such episodes may find a renewed echo in an age when technology encourages intellectual mobs.[49]

There are echoes and connections to much of this in George Orwell's *Nineteen Eighty-Four* and Aldous Huxley's *Brave New World,* which, though considered outrageous by many when they were first published in 1949 and 1932, respectively, have attained an increasing aura of reality as the years go on and our society evolves in disturbing directions. As Julia, a character in *Nineteen Eighty-Four,* says, "Always yell with the crowd, that's what I say. It's the only way to be safe." Even though Julia understands that all she reads and hears from the authorities and from the crowd is *rubbish,* "she knew when to cheer and when to boo, and that was all one needed."[50]

Nineteen Eighty-Four depicts a totalitarian society where the past is always being rewritten to conform with the reigning opinions of the present. The past and the people who populated the past are not allowed to be judged by the standards of their own era, with all of their moral strengths and defects, but only by the rules and standards of today. The past, thus, is in a crucial way eliminated. "Chaucer, Shakespeare, Milton, Byron" are no longer read in the original, but "changed into something contradictory of what they used to be" to suit the demands of the crowd. In fact, there is no past in Orwell's fictional society. "The past was erased, the erasure was forgotten, the lie became truth." All ignorance flowed from this fact, since it is only by knowing what has come before, and the values and assumptions that previous generations used to live by—what worked in those days and what didn't—that any society could have any hope of a mature perspective on its current challenges. Yet, as Orwell tells us, "History has stopped. Nothing exists except an endless present," as one breathless news cycle replaces the next, with no one looking back over their shoulder for any perspective or meaning.[51] Huxley, in *Brave New World*, depicts how "new forms of drunkenness" will enable future society in this "endless present" to exist in a state of partial or permanent tranquilization, subsisting on movies, "gutter journalism," trashy music, and the like.[52] It is the landscape of shattered glass depicted in Eliot's *The Waste Land*.

This is where Spengler and Canetti come together with Orwell and Huxley. By any standards imaginable, the world that Orwell and Huxley describe signifies Spengler's decline of the West and Canetti's tyranny of the crowd. This is all happening and starting to happen before our eyes. We see it in how literature and the liberal arts at large are being dramatically undermined by ideology, so that only one interpretation is allowed; how individualism is being assaulted by fads and trends and viral tweets and videos and such; how a suite of pills are required for even well-balanced and successful people to sleep at night and relax during the day; and how journalism is becoming more ideological on one hand and trashier on the other hand (especially the cable news shows on daytime television). And all this is to say nothing about the looming ability of artificial intelligence, and programmers thereof, to unleash whole new levels of coercive, conformist thinking.

The first among equals in all of this is Canetti's *crowd,* which is the vehicle for both civilizational decline and individual coercion. And it is Canetti, perhaps more than any other modern writer, who has isolated crowd psychology as an intellectual subject all its own. Crowds, as Canetti shows in his description of the "hunting pack," have existed since the dawn of time. Citizens in a well-functioning democracy do not constitute a crowd in the sense that Canetti means, since democracy involves individual choice in the privacy of the voting booth, where the crowd cannot intimidate you since nobody knows in the end which lever you will pull, or which candidate you will check off. Despite all the riotous rallies of the campaign, it comes down to a secret act. And that is to the good. Assuming that the winning majority has reasonable respect for the losing minority, democracy actually demonstrates the limits of crowd coercion. Yet there is still a danger, since modern and postmodern technology—first newspapers and radio, now X and Facebook—has created untold vistas for the tyranny of the crowd. And this can subvert the spirit of democracy. Indeed, we think we are more tolerant and civilized because of technology. But technology and civilization are two different things; not necessarily opposed, but not necessarily in harmony, either. The demons behind World War I and World War II demonstrated how technological advances—the triumphs of industrialization employed for the purposes of war and mass killing—can be conducive to barbarism. Technology can lead to a better world and more efficient democracy, sure. It all depends . . . to repeat, just look at what happened at *The New York Times* in 2020. The tyranny born of an assemblage of people had as its goal the destruction of two liberal individuals who hadn't sufficiently proved their virtue in the eyes of the crowd.

The affair at *The New York Times,* merely one event inside a news cycle of George Floyd–related national drama, points to a pivotal difference between the 20th and 21st centuries. The 20th century was an age of mass communications often controlled by big governments, so that ideology and its attendant intimidation were always delivered from the top down. Hitler, Stalin, and Mao can only be imagined in a 20th-century context against the backdrop of the climax of the Industrial Revolution. The 21st century has produced an inversion of all this, whereby individuals can work through digital networks to gather together from the bottom up. This does not end tyranny from the top down, as we know from present-day Russia and China. But it does add another dimension to the battle in defense of free thought.

Bottom-up crowds will obviously have various effects. They are a force behind bestseller and greatest-hit lists. They can destroy reputations before the full truth emerges. They can reduce the presidential primary system to a contest of demagogues. They demonstrate, as the Founders of the American Revolution knew, that unrestrained democracy is the proving ground of anarchy. But they can also be forces for good. The Arab Spring in 2011 in North Africa and the Middle East may have failed, but it began with hope for a less oppressive political future—and bottom-up crowds forged by social media were the primary cause of that. The uprisings against a brutal clerical regime in Iran in 2009 and 2022 could not have happened without the self-organizing, bottom-up crowd phenomenon of social media. One woman in Tehran in September 2022, Mahsa Amini, was brutalized and killed by so-called morality police for not properly wearing her hijab, and the news spread to this person and that one via social media, and built and built, until vast bottom-up demonstrations nearly rocked the regime in major cities.

The point is that social and digital media in the world-cities will ignite more domestic and geopolitical turbulence, even if it is periodically toward a good end against truly tyrannical regimes. Social media in the world-cities are a key reason why politics will continue to get harder, more complicated, and more difficult to succeed at. It isn't only that highly populated and complex countries like Pakistan, Nigeria, and South Africa in the developing world have increasingly teetered on becoming failed states; rather, it is that it has gotten harder to govern countries like the United States and France, too. The populations in absolute terms get bigger and bigger, if not in every case. The people have more and more demands. Whereas countries of vast and illiterate peasantries can be quite stable, since the population is relatively fatalistic and consequently has fewer claims to make on politicians, the development of literate working and middle classes, though it counts as progress, can lead to instability, since the population is no longer fatalistic and expects more of government. Middle classes are just tougher to govern, something that cannot be helped, especially in democratic societies. This is as true in Nigeria and South Africa as it is in former Communist Central and Eastern Europe. As Samuel P. Huntington bluntly put it, "The faster the enlightenment of the population, the more frequent the overthrow of the government."[53]

It isn't that the world is getting worse. It's getting better. More and more people live fuller and richer lives, and have more and better ways to communicate their feelings. And this makes governing them more difficult, even as they form into virtual crowds that, while professing independence, will operate on the basis of a brutal conformity. For the act of protest is not wholly innocent. It demands that a large group of people think as one in order to be organized. Whole populations, in the grip of some political frenzy or other, tapping feverishly on their smartphones in unison their approval or disapproval, will increasingly resemble the mores of teenage girls, in which the worst fear will be that of ostracism.

The challenge is still one identified by both Canetti and Arendt: individual loneliness and atomization that creates blind obedience to crowds. For the crowd signals a rejection of reality in order to create an alternative reality: something that is doable provided a large number of people believe in it. This is something that technology itself can help with, with possibly frightening consequences. The future will be a contest of crowds: those imposing reality and those demanding a new reality. As for the effect of artificial intelligence on all of this, it will not be a panacea, but may only exacerbate the problem that these timeless philosophers raise. The former secretary of state Henry Kissinger, former Google CEO Eric Schmidt, and MIT College of Computing dean Daniel Huttenlocher wrote in *The Wall Street Journal* that "in the worlds of media, politics, discourse, and entertainment, AI will reshape information to conform to our preferences—potentially confirming and deepening biases, and, in so doing, narrowing access to . . . an objective truth."[54] AI, because of its perceived omnipotence, could make it even harder to challenge acceptable opinion and conventional wisdom, and thus it can become a weapon of the ruling mob, like Google algorithms that not only pick winners and losers but merely amplify the lowest common denominator of popularity in the contest of ideas. AI, rather than a liberator, would in that case be an arm of authoritarianism. Like computing in general, AI's indisputable wonders will be in the fields of medicine, engineering, and other areas of science. But as it concerns democracy and mass society,

AI's effects could be distinctly problematic. An elite few may control AI: a scientific mandarinate answerable to nobody, it will seem, even as AI becomes a third form of consciousness alongside secular thought and religious faith, according to Kissinger, Schmidt, and Huttenlocher.[55] AI could make judgments that, spread by social media, make it even more dangerous for those who wish to stand outside the crowd.

While the tyranny that can be produced by bottom-up social media in many cases has a different style than top-down Industrial Age authoritarianism, it has a similar result: the intimidation of dissent through a professed monopoly on virtue. If you don't agree with us, you are not only wrong but morally wanting, and as such should not only be denounced but destroyed. Remember, both Nazism and Communism were utopian ideologies. In the minds of their believers they were systems of virtue, and precisely because of that they opened up new vistas for tyranny. Despite the passing of Hitler, Stalin, and Mao, tyranny, I repeat, is not done with us. And I am not just talking about Putin, Xi, and the other dictators who plague international relations; I am talking about new and subtler forms of coercion at home.

It is the lust for purity and perfect virtue that, when combined with social media and other forms of communications technology, becomes particularly acute, since it puts power in the hands of the young, who are understandably more adaptable than their elders in the use of new cyber and digital products. This, too, raises the specter of particularly fearsome bottom-up mobs, since the young are not tempered by memories of the past and the grave mistakes they made in that past. The upshot of such crowd coercion is widespread self-censorship: the cornerstone of all forms of totalitarianism. Because the historic West is ultimately about the freedom of the individual to rise above the crowd, Spengler's theory of decline may be right for reasons even he doesn't mention.

Of course, as we've seen, it can work the other way, too. Social media in Iran in the hands of the young can have the possibility of reinventing the West inside a reactionary religious tyranny. So while I am pointing out the dangers of the new technology and new types of crowd formations, I am, nevertheless, aware that it will also lead to positive breakthroughs. But in every case, it will make geopolitics more unpredictable and more tumultuous. Regimes, good and bad, throughout the world will be constantly in danger, contributing to a general anxiety and claustrophobia reminiscent of Weimar, where public life and politics were always in turmoil. And the two are entwined, since everything it seems is political now.

THE DECLINE OF THE WEST began not only with the rise and elaboration of Eliot's bleak, "Unreal" cities, delinked from the soil and beset by crowd frenzy, but with the birth of modernism itself, both of which are themes in *The Waste Land*.[56] Modernism signaled indifference to (and independence from) the past, leading toward what the Marxists called "progress" and away from sacred traditions with their self-imposed limits, a process which encouraged disintegration and extremism. The very word *modern* suggests a dismissal of everything that comes before it as primitive in some way or other. Modernism was a breaking of the rules. Unmoored from the past and its sacred traditions, modern politics reinvented group, ethnic, and religious identities in starker, ideological terms. This counterintuitively released an "instinctual power" over politics—that is, the release of raw emotions—according to the

Princeton historian of turn-of-the-20th-century Vienna, Carl E. Schorske. Remember that Vienna in that period produced not only the disturbing modern art of Gustav Klimt and Oskar Kokoschka, but the psycho-sexual theories of Sigmund Freud, and the ideological, mass-market anti-Semitism of Karl Lueger that would lead in a straight line to Adolf Hitler. "In our [20th] century," Schorske writes, "rational man has had to give place to that richer but more dangerous and mercurial creature, psychological man. This new man is not merely a rational animal, but a creature of feeling and instinct."[57]

Being a creature of feeling and instinct, not only did racial politics, in the modern political sense, rise up under Vienna mayor Karl Lueger, but also under that fierce pan-Germanist and anti-Semite, the Austrian politician Georg von Schönerer. Theodore Herzl, the father of political Zionism and another Viennese personality of the same period, was also, according to Schorske, typical of the time, as Herzl's answer to anti-Semitism was not liberalism, but a national movement built on race and ethnicity, however morally warranted it might have been. Lueger, von Schönerer, and Herzl were all reacting to the loss of a traditional sense of belonging that appealed to a reactionary need for identity. Listen to Schorske:

"... each of these political artists—Schönerer, Lueger, and Herzl—grasped a social-psychological reality which the liberal could not see. Each expressed in politics a rebellion against reason and law which soon became more widespread. In their manner of secession from the liberal political tradition and in the form of the challenge they posed to its values, this triad of politicians adumbrated a concept of life and a mode of action which ... constituted part of the wider cultural revolution that ushered in the twentieth century."[58]

Men and women were not necessarily destined to be liberal. They could also be tribal, defining themselves in modern ideological terms by geography, group, ethnicity, and/or religion. And that has helped lead from the late 19th century onward, picking up steam as it has gone along, to the weakening of Western civilization, since all civilizations rest to a significant degree on the repression of tribal and other instincts (something we know from Freud):[59] since to be civilized is to judge people as individuals, not as members of a race or ethnic group, and also to constantly repress your natural, momentary desires; otherwise you may run afoul of the law or be ejected from polite company.

But civilization is now in flux. The ongoing decay of the West is manifested not only in racial tensions coupled with new barriers to free speech, but in the deterioration of dress codes, the erosion of grammar, the decline in sales of serious books and classical music, and so on, all of which have traditionally been signs of civilization. One might counter that what is happening is merely an evolution of styles, and that society is more democratic because of it, since things like correct grammar and classical music and serious books are only elite conventions that the masses and popular culture reject. That may well be true, but it is precisely such an evolution of styles, and also of media, politics, entertainment, and so on, that register cultural change, which, in turn, can lead to the very decline Spengler speaks of. The West has crested, in other words, and with it has crested the main invention of the West, the sanctity of the individual and individual thought, that is by definition opposed to the crowd. This has been made worse by extreme poverty and social dysfunction within Western societies themselves, condemning groups and the neighborhoods where they live to impoverishment as individuals within those groups. In short, elites are increasingly conformist and the masses, especially the underclass, are more ignorant, as schools and other public services decline.

Of course, many intellectual and journalistic elites believe that Western civilization is giving way over time to a more humane and rules-based global civilization, in which case explosions of primitive behavior—whether mass shootings, war, other atrocities, or extremist politics—may abate somewhat. But just as likely there will be a civilizational vacuum, with anarchy becoming more prevalent. For the mechanization, automation, and routinized bureaucratic procedure imposed by experts (and by science itself) are bound to absolutely enrage a fair number of us, leading to the very loss of repression against instinct that civilization is supposed to impose in the first place. The more constrained we are all forced to be in our behavior and our beliefs, in other words, the more that political extremists, including violent and crazy groups, will seek to overturn the prevailing order.

Such extremists will clash with a populace existing under a strict hierarchy. As the philosophers Friedrich Nietzsche and José Ortega y Gasset warned us, science is conspiring with crowd psychology, wrought, in turn, by urban life, to produce a race of *mass men* in the cities.[60] Mass men can act in a conformist way, even as they believe themselves to be individuals existing above the nation-state. The two things are not necessarily in contradiction. Mass men, who will both rule and compose the urban populace, are heavily credentialed experts within their narrow cubicles of bureaucratic and subject-matter existence, ignorant of what lies outside, and therefore prone to membership in virtual mobs, which are bent on the latest fad, or assaulting in one form or another the next victim and his or her reputation. The very expansion of knowledge creates ever more intense and minute fields of specialization, which drives workers into little cubbyholes of experience, making everything beyond those cubbyholes, aside from immediate psychological and carnal needs, unreal and prone to manipulation by, for example, social-media demagogues. Such phenomena will help define city life of the future; or increasingly of the present, as both Ph.D.s and Internet influencers tell us what to think. This is how the most erudite and scientific minds can fall under the sway of a pop musician, sports figure, or politician. If a bit of nonsense is repeated enough times on a cable news channel, the most educated among us may start to believe it.

Ortega writes in his classic, *The Revolt of the Masses,* that "the direction of society has been taken over by a type of man oblivious to the principles of civilization. . . . He is obviously interested in automobiles, anesthetics, and all manner of sundries. And these things confirm his profound lack of interest in civilization itself." In an introduction to Ortega's book, Saul Bellow observes, "The mass man loves gags. He is a spoilt child, demanding amusement, given to tantrums. . . . His only commandment is, Thou shalt expect convenience." And as Ortega summarizes, mass men "are concerned only with their well-being," while showing "no concern for the causes and reasons for that well-being." Thus, "they imagine that their role is limited to demanding these benefits peremptorily, as if they were natural rights."[61] Owning the latest device is not a natural right; neither is getting delivery of your favorite new product in twenty-four hours, or constantly being entertained in general. These have become things we now expect, but are, in fact, results of a highly evolved and therefore ever more fragile civilization.

This is how civilization eventually dies. It is just such a soporific reality that political extremists will revolt against. In their revolts and upheavals, and in the mass obsessions, political, financial, and sexual, that the mass man will take part in, made vivid by interactive technology, conflict between different parts of the earth will intensify, even as there is an overbearing sameness to the cities of the earth.

Mass men are particularly prone to extreme political ideologies, warned the 20th-century diplomat and foreign policy realist Robert Strausz-Hupé, since ideologies "are mass products in the true sense," and "represent the final, deepest degradation of reason."[62] Crowds, mobs, social conformity, and ideology all flow together, helped by technology. Usually it occurs in cities but periodically in virtual cities created by social media, like the January 6th mob. Despite the metaverse, the range of human experience itself will become increasingly narrow, so that wisdom and good judgment will be even more difficult to come by. The work-from-home phenomenon could intensify some of this, as it separates the wealthier classes from a mask- and glove-wearing servant class that brings parcels to their doors and attends to them at high-end restaurants. This is how pandemics isolate the economic and social classes. The tech industry evangelizes about stretching the boundaries of human experience. But in the future the opposite may turn out to be the case.

For a somewhat oblique picture of what this might look like, consider the perfectly engineered cities of China, built on massive surveillance technology and artificial intelligence, in which AI will keep watch over every city street. In the Chinese vision, both frightening and sleep-inducing, traffic jams will be alleviated, missing children will be quickly found, ambulances will get to their destinations faster, jaywalkers will be shamed, and the government will know your thoughts by way of your Internet searches. Because most people do not concern themselves with the world of ideas, and value safety and convenience above all, the Chinese city may actually represent the ultimate challenge to the less-efficient and mob-prone urban West.[63]

Not too bad, you might say about these Chinese cities. Most people, if not intellectuals, could easily live with such a vision. Indeed, dystopia may only be in the eyes of the beholder.

Yet, as Camus writes in *The Rebel,* it is in man's nature to revolt. "Man's solidarity is founded upon rebellion, and rebellion, in its turn, can only find its justification in this solidarity."[64] That is the conundrum. Control will only get you so far. The more control there is, whether by diversionary spectacles and other amusements, or by all manner of drugs and medications, or by the tyranny of the crowd, or the tyranny of a dictator, the greater may be the eventual reaction against it. The tyranny of the crowd, as we have seen, may be the most insidious of all these tyrannies and, by leading to self-censorship, may be the hardest to rebel against. Still, Ortega's mass man, the ultimate tool of the crowd, may not constitute, according to the cliché, the soporific end of history. For there will always be revolt. And the revolt may come when things go wrong, when life is suddenly not convenient for the mass man. And things periodically do go very wrong. Keep in mind that the ancient Greeks feared chaos because they were too rational themselves to discount what lay on the other side of rationality. It is clear that intermittent chaos is a condition that will not dissipate as science and technology deliver more wonders to humanity. Chaos need not happen strictly on the geopolitical level, when the end of absolutist regimes leads not to stable democracy but to various levels of anarchy and new forms of disorder, as we've learned from the Arab Spring and the mayhem that gripped Russia following the fall of Communism in the 1990s. Chaos can also grip postmodern technological societies, where revolt takes the form of primitive paroxysms, embracing lies or violence or both, in a reaction against soulless technocracy and the tyranny of crowds that demand perfect virtue.

AND BECAUSE ANARCHY IS a permanent condition of the species, which encompasses periodic eruptions of barbarism, ideological movements such as Communism and fascism are never actually dead, but only in occultation. We must always beware of the year *one,* 1917 and 1933.

The late Polish-born Israeli historian Zeev Sternhell defined fascism as, in part, a revolt against "the life of the great cities, which was dominated by routine, with no room for heroism." Fascism, Sternhell went on, was a "true counter-civilization" emphasizing "the rediscovery of instinct"—of our deepest psychological and physical urges. Fascism had a strong romantic appeal, wrote the German-born American historian Walter Laqueur. "Passion was to be a substitute for reason, readiness to fight a substitute for useless sophistic arguments." With fascism there was always this obsession with virility.[65] Fascism, in short, is the bullies' ideology. It is the very soulless, effete, and postmodern urban civilization that has been growing up all around us that, it turns out, may provide fertile soil for fascism, by providing it with an environment it can rally against. Communism, too, or some variation of it, may find a sort of rebirth, only because it idealizes the romantic and seemingly virtuous left-wing extreme, and is thus suited to the 21st-century crowd. My point is that the more conformist postmodern urban civilization forces us to become, the more often we will face revolts from the new-old zealotry of the Right and Left.

Remember that totalitarianism itself is rooted in a perversion of Western thought, according to the great Harvard thinkers of the

1950s Zbigniew Brzezinski and Carl Friedrich. "For example," as they point out, "the idea of progress, so peculiar a product of the Western mind, is embedded in the totalitarian thought so deeply that it would collapse if this idea were eliminated."[66] Of course, when liberals and neoconservatives talk of *progress*, they mean something vastly different than when Nazis and Communists do. But the concept is the same: believing in a linear forward direction to history, which, by definition, is not tragic. That is, it does not admit to the tendency of things to go wrong—does not admit to ironic outcomes—but always aims in the direction of utopia.

So what of the West, at least as we revere it, obviously without the perversions of totalitarian ideologies? What about the survival of individual thought? The yearning to escape from the crowd? For that is what the West, in the healthiest sense, is ultimately about, and what throughout the centuries has given Western civilization its peculiar power and dynamism. The West wrested the individual from the group, gave him or her autonomy, and thus gave birth to freedom.

The brilliant 19th-century Russian intellectual Alexander Herzen, anticipating Spengler and writing in the wake of the failed 1848 democratic revolutions in Europe, delivered perhaps the most pessimistic of warnings:

"Modern Western thought will pass into history and be incorporated in it, will have its influence and its place, just as our body will pass into the composition of grass, of sheep, of cutlets, and of men. We do not like that kind of immortality, but what is to be done about it?"[67]

That is, the West will gradually pass away.

Herzen then widens his canvas:

"After the break-up of Rome came Christianity; after Christianity, the belief in civilization, in humanity. Liberalism is the final *religion,* though its church is not of the other world but of this." And liberalism, the finest achievement of the West, Herzen implies, will end up as one of modern man's "shattered idols." In this way, his vision is akin to T. S. Eliot's.[68]

This is what we are up against—again, the natural process of history that will undermine and dilute the West, and all it stands for. As globalization naturally plunges the West into the crosscurrents of other civilizations, and extreme forms of identity politics trample the rights of the individual, historic liberalism now has the task of infinitely postponing Herzen's vision. Historic liberalism—exemplified by thinkers such as Edmund Burke, John Stuart Mill, and Isaiah Berlin—as the champion of individual agency and of an open mind, offers the ultimate rebuke to the crowd. Historic liberalism has as its root the willingness to entertain reasonable ideas different from one's own. Liberalism "is not too sure that it is right," said the great jurist Learned Hand.[69] Modern conservatives fit within this category, too, since they aim to *conserve* what is best in Western liberal thought (something that will be particularly challenging in an age of uncontrolled artificial intelligence). Liberalism thus delivers a critique to extremist ideologies like fascism and Communism, and to the fate Herzen had in mind. Combatting the folk and the mob, cultivating moderation in both foreign and domestic policy amid incipient global anarchy and roiling geopolitics caused by the decline of the great powers, is at root about being a liberal. This is certainly not new, but in the face of all the material I have presented it *is* poignant.

That said, even liberals must realize their philosophy's own limitations, and thus not be overly zealous. Because liberalism, on account of its focus on individual rights, taken to an extreme, can ultimately mean the erasure of "borders and boundaries based in geography, history, and nature," writes Notre Dame political scientist Patrick Deneen.[70] Indeed, liberals must seek their ends in moderation, or else national cultures themselves are threatened by individual rights run amok. Liberalism must not hate all soil ties, I mean, or else incur the wrath of Spengler and his dark declinist vision. After all, a pure cosmopolitanism, by rejecting any closed geographical space where democracy has always flourished, can itself be anti-democratic.[71]

That is why we must always remember 1848, the year of the failed democratic revolutions across Europe, when liberalism and nationalism actually "fought on the same side of the barricades," writes Robert Strausz-Hupé.[72] The failure of those revolutions was not preordained, however, but was a matter of many tenuous contingencies. Had the 1848 revolutions succeeded—which they almost did—there might have been no World War I and following that no Hitler. History, once again, is a series of hinges. Even if the trends are bad, as I have certainly enumerated, better and worse outcomes are always available. Indeed, precisely because Spengler's historical perspective is so long and broad, urban civilization, as we know it, may yet find renewal and have more miles to run.

OXFORD UNIVERSITY PHILOSOPHER William MacAskill writes that "we stand at the beginning of history. For every person alive today, ten have lived and died in the past. But if human beings survive as long as the average mammal species, then for every person alive today, a thousand people will live in the future. We are the ancients. On the scale of a typical human life, humanity today is barely an infant struggling to walk."[73]

By that time frame my relentlessly pessimistic argument is fleeting. Whole new cycles of history await that will overwhelm everything that I have just written. But that does not mean that what

I have written does not matter. Humanity may go on for tens of thousands of years, or it may destroy itself in short order. And even if it goes on, it is unclear how free and unprogrammed by machines human beings will be. Can we reclaim the true freedom and diversity of Jane Jacobs's sidewalk?

The direction of history is unknowable. There is no such thing as automatic linear progress. Thus, we have no choice but to fight on, as the outcome is not given to any of us in advance. Weimar boasted many liberals and a true intellectual flowering. There was much hope in Weimar, but insufficient order. Avoiding Weimar's fate now constitutes the ultimate labor for the world.

ACKNOWLEDGMENTS

THIS BOOK COULD NOT HAVE BEEN DONE WITHOUT THE SUPPORT of the Foreign Policy Research Institute (FPRI) in Philadelphia. For this I thank FPRI's president emerita, Carol "Rollie" Flynn; its president, Aaron Stein; and the chairman of the board of trustees, Robert L. Freedman.

Molly Turpin at Random House was an invaluable and delightful editor. Henry Thayer, Marianne Merola, and the rest of the team at Brandt & Hochman Literary Agents continue to represent me in the best sense of old-fashioned virtue.

Elizabeth M. Lockyer has managed my professional life for decades now, and without her assistance in so many ways this book would not have been possible. Maria Cabral, my wife of forty-one years, provided the love, stability, and understanding necessary for this book and all my others.

Parts of this manuscript first appeared in the editorial pages of *The Wall Street Journal,* and in *The New Criterion, The National Interest,* and *The New Statesman,* for which I thank the editors.

NOTES

1. WEIMAR GOES GLOBAL

1. Christopher Isherwood, *The Berlin Stories,* including *Goodbye to Berlin.* New York: New Directions, (1939) 2008, pp. 207, 343, 389.
2. Gordon A. Craig, *Germany: 1866–1945.* New York: Oxford University Press, (1978) 1987, p. 483.
3. Alfred Döblin, *Berlin Alexanderplatz.* Trans. Michael Hofmann. New York: Penguin, (1929) 2019, pp. 70, 113, 440.
4. Golo Mann, *The History of Germany Since 1789.* Trans. Marian Jackson. New York: Penguin Books, 1968, p. 681.
5. Craig, *Germany,* p. 434.
6. Mann, *The History of Germany Since 1789,* p. 586.
7. "Beer Hall Putsch," Encyclopedia of the United States Holocaust Memorial Museum, Washington. David King, *The Trial of Adolf Hitler: The Beer Hall Putsch and the Rise of Nazi Germany.* New York: W. W. Norton & Company, 2017, p. 101.
8. Craig, *Germany,* p. 540.
9. Mann, *The History of Germany Since 1789,* pp. 664, 673–75. Craig, *Germany,* p. 568.
10. Modris Eksteins, *Rites of Spring: The Great War and the Birth of the Modern Age.* Boston: Houghton Mifflin, 1989, p. 301.
11. Richard M. Langworth, *Churchill by Himself: The Definitive Collection of Quotations.* New York: PublicAffairs, 2011, from April 26, 1945.
12. Henry Kissinger, *A World Restored: Metternich, Castlereagh and the Problems of Peace 1812–22.* Boston: Houghton Mifflin reprint (1957), p. 283. Rob-

ert D. Kaplan, "Kissinger, Metternich, and Realism." Boston: *The Atlantic,* June 1999.
13. Reinhold Niebuhr, *The Irony of American History.* New York: Charles Scribner's Sons, 1952, p. 78 of 2008 University of Chicago Press edition.
14. Aleksandr Solzhenitsyn, *August 1914.* Trans. Michael Glenny. New York: Farrar, Straus and Giroux, 1971, pp. 100, 405.
15. Solzhenitsyn, *August 1914,* pp. 13, 57, 59.
16. Solzhenitsyn, *August 1914,* pp. 130–31, 134.
17. Solzhenitsyn, *August 1914,* p. 357.
18. Aleksandr Solzhenitsyn, *November 1916: The Red Wheel, Node II.* Trans. H. T. Willetts. New York: Farrar, Straus and Giroux, (1984) 1999, p. 214.
19. Aleksandr Solzhenitsyn, *March 1917: The Red Wheel, Node III, Book 3.* Trans. Marian Schwartz. Notre Dame, Indiana: University of Notre Dame Press, English language edition 2021, pp. 230, 387.
20. Solzhenitsyn, *November 1916,* p. 905.
21. Joseph Conrad, *Under Western Eyes.* Introduction and Notes by Boris Ford. New York: Penguin Books, (1911) 1985, pp. 9, 105.
22. Solzhenitsyn, *November 1916,* p. 653.
23. John Reed, *The Collected Works of John Reed.* New York: The Modern Library, (1919) 1995, p. 717.
24. A. J. P. Taylor, Introduction to John Reed, *Ten Days That Shook the World.* New York: Penguin Books, 1977, p. xvi.
25. Aleksandr Solzhenitsyn, *March 1917, Node III, Book 1.* Trans. Marian Schwartz. Notre Dame, Indiana: University of Notre Dame Press, 1986 and 2008, pp. 154–55.
26. Daniel J. Mahoney, "Solzhenitsyn's *Red Wheel:* The Russian Author's Crowning Achievement Defends a Tough-Minded Christianity." New York: *First Things,* May 2015.
27. Solzhenitsyn, *March 1917: The Red Wheel, Node III, Book 3,* p. 127.
28. Sean McMeekin, *The Russian Revolution: A New History.* New York: Basic Books, 2017, p. 267. Costica Bradatan, *In Praise of Failure: Four Lessons in Humility.* Cambridge, Massachusetts: Harvard University Press, 2023, p. 103.
29. Kissinger, *A World Restored,* p. 206.
30. Ann Applebaum, *Iron Curtain: The Crushing of Eastern Europe 1944–1956.* New York: Doubleday, 2012, p. 383.
31. David Guaspari, "Here's Johnny: A Review of 'The Man from the Future: The Visionary Life of John von Neumann' by Ananyo Bhattacharya." New York: *The New Criterion,* October 2022.
32. Paul Bracken, *Fire in the East: The Rise of Asian Military Power and the Second Nuclear Age.* New York: HarperCollins, 1999, p. 33.
33. Halford Mackinder, "The Geographical Pivot of History." London: *The Geographical Journal,* April 1904, p. 422.

NOTES

34. Adam Tooze, "Chartbook 130 Defining Polycrisis—From Crisis Pictures to the Crisis Matrix," http://AdamTooze.com/category/blog.
35. Cliff Kupchan, "Ukrainian Fallout." Washington: *The National Interest*, November/December 2022.
36. Henry Kissinger, Eric Schmidt, and Daniel Huttenlocher, *The Age of AI: And Our Human Future*. New York: Little, Brown, 2021, p. 152.
37. Colin S. Gray, *Another Bloody Century: Future Warfare*. London: Weidenfeld & Nicolson, 2005, p. 34.
38. Kissinger, *Nuclear Weapons and Foreign Policy*, New York: Doubleday Anchor Books, 1957, pp. 140, 148.
39. Robert D. Kaplan, "Kennan's Containment Strategy: A Consensus on What Not to Do." Washington: *The National Interest*, April 24, 2021.
40. Kissinger, *Nuclear Weapons and Foreign Policy*, pp. 43, 45–46, 56, 57, 59.
41. Timothy Snyder, "War No More: Why the World Has Become More Peaceful." New York: *Foreign Affairs*, January/February 2012.
42. Robert D. Kaplan, "Has Violence Declined?" Austin, Texas: Stratfor, July 11, 2012.
43. Gray, *Another Bloody Century*, p. 29.
44. Gray, *Another Bloody Century*, pp. 15, 95.
45. Ralph Peters, *Fighting for the Future: Will America Triumph?* Mechanicsburg, Pennsylvania: Stackpole Books, 1999, p. 171.
46. Martin van Creveld, *The Transformation of War*. New York: The Free Press, 1991, p. 161.
47. Peter Brannen, "The Terrifying Warning Lurking in the Earth's Ancient Rock Record." Washington: *The Atlantic*, February 11, 2021.
48. Brannen, "The Terrifying Warning Lurking in the Earth's Ancient Rock Record."
49. Robert D. Kaplan, *Warrior Politics: Why Leadership Demands a Pagan Ethos*. New York: Random House, 2002, chap. 7.
50. Daniel Yergin, "Net Zero." New York: *The Wall Street Journal*, April 12, 2023.
51. Paul Theroux, *The Last Train to Zona Verde: My Ultimate African Safari*. New York: Houghton Mifflin Harcourt, 2013, pp. 8, 17, 201, 297–98, 345.
52. Theroux, *The Last Train to Zona Verde*, p. 337.
53. Janan Ganesh, "Anarchy Is a Likelier Future for the West Than Tyranny." London: *Financial Times*, June 21, 2022.
54. Gérard Prunier, *Africa's World War: Congo, the Rwandan Genocide, and the Making of a Continental Catastrophe*. New York: Oxford University Press, 2009, pp. xxix–xxx.
55. Robert D. Kaplan, "The Anarchy That Came." Washington: *The National Interest*, October 21, 2018.

11. THE GREAT POWERS IN DECLINE

1. Henry Adams, *The Education of Henry Adams: An Autobiography*. Introduction by Edmund Morris. New York: The Modern Library, (1907 and 1918) 1996, pp. 44, 438–39.
2. Barbara W. Tuchman, *The Guns of August*. New York: Macmillan (Dell reprint), 1962, pp. 345–46.
3. Robert Conquest, *The Harvest of Sorrow: Soviet Collectivization and the Terror-Famine*. New York: Oxford University Press, 1986, p. 3.
4. Antony Beevor, *Stalingrad: The Fateful Siege: 1942–1943*. New York: Penguin Books, 1998, pp. 85, 166–67.
5. Stephen F. Cohen, *Failed Crusade: America and the Tragedy of Post-Communist Russia*. New York: W. W. Norton & Company, 2000, pp. 3, 5, 7–9, 11.
6. Steven Lee Myers, *The New Tsar: The Rise and Reign of Vladimir Putin*. New York: Knopf, 2015, p. 92.
7. Jakub Grygiel, "Ukraine War Shows the 'Rules-Based International Order' Is a Myth." New York: *The Wall Street Journal,* March 28, 2022.
8. "Seriously wounded" in this case means either the loss of at least one major limb or one or both eyes, or serious burns on the face. This emerged from a 2010 study by the Center for a New American Security in Washington. Robert D. Kaplan, "The Wounded Home Front." Washington: *The American Interest,* February 2011.
9. Nancy Mitford, *Frederick the Great*. London: Random House and Vintage, (1970) 2011, p. 182.
10. Aleksandr Solzhenitsyn, *One Day in the Life of Ivan Denisovich*. Trans. H. T. Willetts. Introduction by John Bayley. New York: Everyman's Library, (1962) 1995, pp. xii, 60–61.
11. Paul Kennedy, *Victory at Sea: Naval Power and the Transformation of the Global Order in World War II*. New Haven, Connecticut: Yale University Press, 2022, p. 408. Kennedy quotes Correlli Barnett as calling great wars the "auditors" of all things.
12. Robert Blake, *Disraeli*. New York: St. Martin's Press, 1967.
13. Ezra F. Vogel, *Deng Xiaoping: And the Transformation of China*. Cambridge, Massachusetts: Harvard University Press, 2011, pp. 3, 5, 14.
14. Vogel, *Deng Xiaoping,* p. 377.
15. Vogel, *Deng Xiaoping,* p. 475.
16. Vogel, *Deng Xiaoping,* p. 638.
17. Matt Pottinger, Matthew Johnson, and David Feith, "Xi Jinping in His Own Words: What China's Leader Wants—and How to Stop Him from Getting It." New York: *Foreign Affairs,* November 30, 2022.
18. Kevin Rudd, "Xi Jinping Scrambles as China's Economy Stumbles." New York: *The Wall Street Journal,* May 10, 2022.
19. Patty-Jane Geller, "Like It or Not, the U.S. Is in an Arms Race with China." New York: *The Wall Street Journal,* February 16, 2023.

NOTES

20. Jason Willick, "The Grand Strategy Behind Japan's Defense Buildup." *The Washington Post,* December 23, 2022. Robert D. Kaplan, "The Biden Administration Just Stalled China's Advance in the Indo-Pacific." *The Washington Post,* September 21, 2021.
21. I also wrote about the emergence of a common Eurasian maritime system, through the convergence of the Indian and Western Pacific oceans, in my book *Monsoon* (2010), published eight years before the Pentagon renamed Pacific Command as Indo-Pacific Command.
22. Jonathan Holslag, "Neighborhood-First: A Geopolitical Compass for Europe's Military Posture." Brussels, 2023.
23. Annamaria Kiaga and Vicky Leung, "The Transition from the Informal to the Formal Economy in Africa." Geneva: ILO, 2020, p. 13.

III. CROWDS AND CHAOS

1. Joel Kotkin, *The Human City: Urbanism for the Rest of Us*. Evanston, Illinois: Agate Publishing, 2016, p. 51.
2. Jane Jacobs, *The Death and Life of Great American Cities*. New York: Random House, 1961; and the Modern Library, 1993, pp. 37–38, 95, 158, 169, 244–45.
3. Dennis R. Judd and Todd Swanstrom, *City Politics: Private Power and Public Policy*. New York: HarperCollins College Publishers, 1994, pp. 1–3.
4. Robert Lowell, "For the Union Dead." New York: Farrar, Straus and Giroux, 1960.
5. Edmund Wilson, "The Poetry of Drouth." New York: *The Dial,* December 1922.
6. Dominic Green, *The Religious Revolution: The Birth of Modern Spirituality, 1848–1898*. New York: Farrar, Straus and Giroux, 2022, p. 34.
7. Witold Rybczynski, *Makeshift Metropolis: Ideas About Cities*. New York: Scribner, 2010, p. xiii.
8. Kotkin, *The Human City,* p. 39.
9. Richard Florida, *The New Urban Crisis: How Our Cities Are Increasing Inequality, Deepening Segregation, and Failing the Middle Class—and What We Can Do About It*. New York: Basic Books, 2017, pp. 13–14, 33, 98.
10. Kotkin, *The Human City,* pp. 97, 105.
11. Roger Scruton, *The Uses of Pessimism: And the Danger of False Hope*. New York: Oxford University Press, 2010, pp. 142, 145. Roger Scruton, *Gentle Regrets: Thoughts from a Life*. New York: Continuum, 2005, p. 39.
12. Ross Douthat, "American Teens Are Really Miserable. Why?" *The New York Times,* February 18, 2023.
13. Green, *The Religious Revolution,* p. 40.
14. Aleksander Wat, *My Century: The Odyssey of a Polish Intellectual*. Trans. Richard Lourie. Foreword by Czeslaw Milosz. New York Review of Books, 1977 and 1988, pp. 21, 92. Robert D. Kaplan, "The Great Danger

of a New Utopianism." Washington: *The American Interest,* November/December 2015.
15. Kaplan, "The Great Danger of a New Utopianism."
16. Oswald Spengler, *The Decline of the West.* Trans. Charles Francis Atkinson. New York: Vintage Books, (1918 and 1922) 2006, pp. 25, 250–51.
17. Barton Swain, "The Weekend Interview [with Gary Saul Morson]: Violent Protest and the Intelligentsia." New York: *The Wall Street Journal,* June 5, 2020.
18. Hannah Arendt, *The Origins of Totalitarianism.* Oxford, England: Benediction Classics, (1951) 2009, pp. 476–78.
19. Erik Wemple, "James Bennet Was Right." *The Washington Post,* October 27, 2022. Bennet originally made the comments to *Semafor.* Ben Smith, "Inside the Identity Crisis at The New York Times." New York: *Semafor,* October 18, 2022.
20. Jonathan Chait, "James Bennet's Firing Was Just One of Many Illiberal Errors." *New York,* November 1, 2022.
21. Spengler, *The Decline of the West,* pp. 389, 395.
22. Robert D. Kaplan, "Everything Here Is Fake." *The Washington Post,* March 2, 2018.
23. Kaplan, "Everything Here Is Fake."
24. Ibn Khaldun, *The Muqaddimah: An Introduction to History.* Trans. Franz Rosenthal. Princeton, New Jersey: Princeton University Press, (1958) 1989, pp. 93, 109, 133, 136, 140.
25. Spengler, *The Decline of the West,* pp. 20, 24.
26. F. Scott Fitzgerald, *The Great Gatsby.* New York: Charles Scribner's Sons, 1925, p. 182.
27. Scruton, *Gentle Regrets,* p. 39.
28. Spengler, *The Decline of the West,* p. xvi.
29. Robert W. Merry, "Spengler's Ominous Prophecy." Washington: *The National Interest,* January 2, 2013.
30. Spengler, *The Decline of the West,* pp. 104–5, 121, 158, 324.
31. Modris Eksteins, *Rites of Spring: The Great War and the Birth of the Modern Age.* Boston: Houghton Mifflin, 1989, p. 50.
32. T. S. Eliot, "London Letter." New York: *The Dial,* June 1921. Reprinted in the Norton Critical Edition of T. S. Eliot's *The Waste Land.* New York: Norton & Company, 2001, pp. 132–33.
33. James Matthew Wilson, "T. S. Eliot's Still Point." New York: *The New Criterion,* April 2023.
34. Rainer Maria Rilke, *His Last Friendship: Unpublished Letters to Mrs. Eloui Bey.* With a Study by Edmond Jaloux and an Introduction by Marcel Raval. New York: Philosophical Library, 1952, p. 26.
35. F. R. Leavis, *New Bearings in English Poetry.* London: Chatto and Windus, 1932, pp. 90–113. Reprinted in the Norton Critical Edition of *The Waste Land,* p. 174.

NOTES

36. James Parker, "T. S. Eliot Saw All This Coming: One Hundred Years After the Publication of 'The Waste Land,' Its Vision Has Never Been More Terrifying." Washington: *The Atlantic,* January/February 2023.
37. T. S. Eliot, *The Waste Land,* lines 20, 22, 62–63, 368, 430.
38. T. S. Eliot, *The Waste Land,* line 376. Leavis, "The Significance of the Modern Waste Land," p. 183 of the Norton Critical Edition.
39. Delmore Schwartz, "T. S. Eliot as the International Hero," p. 215 of the Norton Critical Edition.
40. Hayden Carruth, Introduction to Jean-Paul Sartre, *Nausea.* New York: New Directions, (1959) 1964.
41. Florida, *The New Urban Crisis,* p. 169. Brandon Fuller and Paul Romer, "Urbanization as Opportunity." Washington: The World Bank, 2013.
42. Solzhenitsyn, *March 1917, Book 1,* p. 88.
43. Aleksandr Solzhenitsyn, *The Red Wheel: March 1917, Node III, Book 2.* Trans. Marian Schwartz. Notre Dame, Indiana: University of Notre Dame Press, 2008, p. 197.
44. Max Hayward, Introduction to *Poems of Akhmatova.* Boston: Houghton Mifflin, 1967, p. 11.
45. Elias Canetti, *Auto-da-Fé.* Trans. C. V. Wedgwood. New York: Farrar, Straus and Giroux, (1935 and 1947) 1984, pp. 15, 17, 66.
46. Elias Canetti, *Crowds and Power.* Trans. Carol Stewart. New York: Penguin Books, (1960) 1981, pp. 15–16, 32.
47. Canetti, *Crowds and Power,* pp. 55–56, 57, 66, 109, 137, 214–220.
48. Canetti, *Crowds and Power,* pp. 331–33.
49. For a blow-by-blow account of the McCarthy era, a little-known biography presents much of the most horrifying material: Robert P. Newman, *Owen Lattimore and the "Loss" of China.* Berkeley, California: University of California Press, 1992.
50. George Orwell, *Nineteen Eighty-Four.* New York: Everyman's Library, (1949) 1982, pp. 128, 163.
51. Orwell, *Nineteen Eighty-Four,* pp. 37, 56, 78, 162.
52. Aldous Huxley, *Brave New World.* Introduction by John Sutherland. New York: Everyman's Library, (1932) 2013, pp. xi, xxiii.
53. Samuel P. Huntington, *Political Order in Changing Societies.* New Haven, Connecticut: Yale University Press, 1968, p. 47.
54. Henry Kissinger, Eric Schmidt, and Daniel Huttenlocher, "ChatGPT Heralds an Intellectual Revolution." New York: *The Wall Street Journal,* February 25, 2023.
55. Henry A. Kissinger, Eric Schmidt, and Daniel Huttenlocher, *The Age of AI: And Our Human Future.* New York: Little, Brown, 2021, p. 208.
56. Eliot, *The Waste Land,* Norton Critical Edition, pp. 7, 12, 18 (lines 60, 207, 376).
57. Carl E. Schorske, *Fin-de-Siècle Vienna: Politics and Culture.* New York: Knopf, 1980, pp. xvii, 4, 118, 251.

58. Schorske, *Fin-de-Siècle Vienna*, p. 120.
59. See Christopher Hitchens, Introduction to Sigmund Freud, *Civilization and Its Discontents*. New York: W. W. Norton & Company, (1930) 2010.
60. See José Ortega y Gasset, *The Revolt of the Masses*. Trans. Anthony Kerrigan. Introduction by Saul Bellow. Notre Dame, Indiana: University of Notre Dame Press, (1930) 1985; and Golo Mann's discussion of Nietzsche in *The History of Germany Since 1789* (1968).
61. José Ortega y Gasset's *The Revolt of the Masses* (1929), pp. xi, 48, 69.
62. Robert Strausz-Hupé, *The Zone of Indifference*. New York: G. P. Putnam's Sons, 1952, p. 136. Alfred Weber, *Farewell to European History*. New Haven, Connecticut: Yale University Press, 1948, pp. 68–71.
63. Josh Chin and Liza Lin, "The Two Faces of China's Surveillance State." New York: *The Wall Street Journal*, September 2, 2022.
64. Albert Camus, *The Rebel: An Essay on Man in Revolt*. Trans. Anthony Bower. New York: Vintage International, (1951) 1991, p. 22.
65. Zeev Sternhell, "Fascist Ideology," in *Fascism: A Reader's Guide: Analyses, Interpretations, Bibliography*, ed. Walter Laqueur. New York: Penguin Books, (1976) 1979, pp. 54, 56, 334, 358–59, 370.
66. Carl J. Friedrich and Zbigniew Brzezinski, *Totalitarian Dictatorship and Autocracy*. Cambridge, Massachusetts: Harvard University Press, 1956, pp. 80–81.
67. Alexander Herzen, *My Past and Thoughts*. Trans. Constance Garnett. Abridged by Dwight Macdonald. Berkeley, California: University of California Press, (1855) 1973, p. 390.
68. Herzen, *My Past and Thoughts*, p. 386.
69. Learned Hand, *The Spirit of Liberty*. New York: Knopf, 1952, p. 190.
70. Patrick J. Deneen, *Why Liberalism Failed: With a New Preface*. New Haven, Connecticut: Yale University Press, 2019, p. xviii.
71. Michael Walzer, *The Struggle for a Decent Politics: On "Liberal" as an Adjective*. New Haven, Connecticut: Yale University Press, 2023, pp. 58–59.
72. Strausz-Hupé, *The Zone of Indifference*, p. 215.
73. William MacAskill, "The Beginning of History: Surviving the Era of Catastrophic Risk." New York: *Foreign Affairs*, September/October 2022.

INDEX

Adams, Henry, 69–70, 72, 73, 75, 76, 79, 80
Adams, John, 69
Adams, John Quincy, 69
Aegis Combat System, 47
Afghanistan
  Soviet invasion of, 101–2, 125
  U.S. war in, 77–78, 87, 91, 92, 153
  U.S. withdrawal from, 80
Africa, 10, 38, 61–62, 65–68. *See also specific countries*
  armed conflicts in, 57–58, 62
  Britain and, 16, 37
  "The Coming Anarchy," 62–68, 162–63
  populations of, 67–68, 122, 123–24, 162–63
  resource scarcity, 63–64, 67
Age of Exploration, 56
agriculture revolution, 56
alienation, 6, 25
Al Qaeda, 55, 77–78
American leadership, deterioration of, 92–95

American Revolution, 137, 171
Amini, Mahsa, 171–72
analogies, 7
anarchy, 8, 11, 19, 20, 26, 32, 79, 108, 182
  "The Coming Anarchy," 62–68, 162–63
Angell, Norman, 54
An Lushan Revolt, 53
Annan, Kofi, 84
Another Bloody Century (Gray), 55–57
anti-Semitism, 124–27, 145, 167, 176
anxiety, 160–61, 175
Arab Spring, 66, 171, 181
architecture, 132–35
Arendt, Hannah, 142, 165, 173
artificial intelligence (AI), 41, 79, 105, 138, 169–70, 173–74, 180–81
arts, 154–60
Asia Society, 115
Atlantic, The, 62, 65
Atlantic Alliance, 121
"Atlantic combine," 73

INDEX

atomic bombing of Hiroshima and Nagasaki, 45
atomization, 173
attack on Pearl Harbor, 73, 77
August 1914 (Solzhenitsyn), 20, 23–28
Australia, 116
authoritarianism, 13, 87–88, 107–8, 115, 173, 174
Auto-da-Fé (Canetti), 165
automation, 92, 178

Bagehot, Walter, 18
"baiting crowd," 166–67
balance of power, 81
Balkan Wars, 41, 51, 74, 77, 80–81, 105–6, 120, 121
Ban Ki-moon, 84
base case scenario, 120–21
Battle of Stalingrad, 73, 95–96
Battle of Tannenberg, 23–27, 71–72
Battle of the Philippine Sea, 41
Bauhaus, 5
Bavarian nationalism, 11
Bedouins, 147–48
Beer Hall Putsch, 10–12, 15
Beethoven, Ludwig van, 155
Beevor, Antony, 96
Bellow, Saul, 179
Bennet, James, 142–43
Berlin, 3–5, 11, 13–14, 17, 70, 80
Berlin, Isaiah, 184
Berlin Alexanderplatz (Döblin), 4–5
Berlin Wall, 74
Bernstein, Leonard, 155
Better Angels of Our Nature, The (Pinker), 53–56
Biden, Joe, 45, 49, 80, 92–93, 106, 127
bin Laden, Osama, 54, 55
bipolar world, 124–27
Bismarck, Otto von, 8, 10, 12
Black Shirts, 13

Bolshevik Revolution. *See* Russian Revolution
Bosnian War, 77
Boston, 131, 133
Bracken, Paul, 37
Brannen, Peter, 59–60
Brave New World (Huxley), 168–69
Brazil, 88
Bremmer, Ian, 38
Brezhnev, Leonid, 91, 125
Brooklyn, 94–95, 132, 133
Brown Shirts, 13
Brueghel, Pieter, the Elder, 23
Brüning, Heinrich, 12–13
Brzezinski, Zbigniew, 182–83
Bulgaria, 74
Bürgerbräu Keller (Munich), 10–11
Burke, Edmund, 112, 184
Buryatia, 128
Bush, George H. W., 93, 106
Bush, George W., 77, 87, 92, 93, 98, 108

Camus, Albert, 159–60, 181
Canada, 58, 94
cancel culture, 141–44
Canetti, Elias, 164–70, 173
capitalism, 75, 76, 111–12
Capitol attack of 2021, 89, 180
carbon dioxide, 59
Carlson, Tucker, 140
Carlyle, Thomas, 131, 132
Carruth, Hayden, 160
Carter, Jimmy, 103
Castro, Fidel, 83
Cavendish, Vermont, 19–20, 135
Ceaușescu, Nicolae, 164
Cezanne, Paul, 155
Chait, Jonathan, 143–44
Chamberlain, Neville, 79
chaos, 66, 108, 119–20, 181–82

INDEX

China, 78, 109–19
  artificial intelligence and, 180–81
  Covid-19 and, 114, 115, 144, 146
  Cultural Revolution, 110–11, 163
  cyberattacks, 42–43, 117
  decline of, 91, 94, 109–19, 122–23
  Hong Kong and, 89
  interconnectedness and, 7, 39, 41–42
  modernizing dictatorship of, 18, 19, 108, 113, 146
  population, 110, 118, 161
  Taiwan and, 39, 41–42, 48–49, 82, 89, 91, 116, 119
  Ukraine War and, 41–42, 125
  U.S. relations with, 41–43, 48–49, 52, 55–56, 92, 94, 112–13, 117–18, 125, 153, 168
Chinese Communist Party, 110–11, 113–14
Christian Democratic Union, 97
Christianity, 183
Churchill, Winston, 14–15, 17, 32, 109
cities, 129–38, 148–52, 161–64
"civilization," Spengler on, 148
"clash of civilizations," 124
claustrophobia, 6, 38, 47, 63, 90, 123–24
climate change, 9, 36, 39, 56, 58, 59–60, 67, 68, 105, 123
climate migration, 67, 122
Clinton, Bill, 75–76, 87, 93
closeness, 34
Cohen, Stephen F., 75–76
Cold War, 16, 38, 41, 42, 44, 47, 49, 50, 62, 73–74, 84–87, 91, 101, 118
"Coming Anarchy, The" (Kaplan), 62–68, 162–63
communism, 27, 33, 100–105, 111–12, 137, 140, 141–42, 149–50, 164
conformity, 133, 140, 163, 165–66, 170, 172–73, 177–78, 180

Congo, 58
connectedness, 6–7, 14, 34, 38–42
Conquest, Robert, 72
Conrad, Joseph, 29
consciousness, 160, 174
conspiracy theories, 140
Constitution, U.S., 8
cosmopolitanism, 15, 135–36, 139, 148–49, 185
Côte d'Ivoire coup d'état of 1999, 65, 66
Cotton, Tom, 142–43
Covid-19 pandemic, 9, 36, 39, 40, 88–89, 142, 180
  China and, 114, 115, 144, 146
  origins of, 144
Craig, Gordon A., 9, 12
Crimea, 51, 79, 82, 97, 105
crowds (crowd psychology), 132, 134–37, 160–61, 163–75. *See also* mobs
  tyranny of the, 167–71
Crowds and Power (Canetti), 164–70, 173
Cuba, 83
Cuban Missile Crisis, 118, 125
Cultural Revolution, 110–11, 163
cyberattacks, 42–43, 68, 95, 117
cyber warfare, 42–43, 79, 87, 160
Czechoslovakia, 74

Dagestan, 126
Dao, James, 142
Death and Life of Great American Cities, The (Jacobs), 130–34, 150, 161, 186
Debussy, Claude, 155
Decline of the West, The (Spengler), 139–40, 144–58, 165, 169, 175, 177
deglobalization, 40, 89
democracy, 5, 11–12, 17–18
Deneen, Patrick, 184–85

199

INDEX

Deng Pufang, 111
Deng Xiaoping, 109–13, 115, 117
deregulation, 76
determinism, 60, 62
Dickens, Charles, 131
"Dictatorships and Double Standards" (Kirkpatrick), 103–5, 108
Dien Bien Phu, 49
digital mobs, 142–44, 161, 163, 170–71
Döblin, Alfred, 3, 4–5, 11
doom, 5
Douthat, Ross, 136

Eastern Question, 107, 108–9
East Germany, 74, 96
Eban, Abba, 83
Ebola, 66
education, 54, 107, 139, 154
Education of Henry Adams, The (Adams), 69–70
Egypt, 83, 123, 125
Einstein, Albert, 109
Eisenhower, Dwight, 48–49, 93
Eksteins, Modris, 157
Eliot, T. S., 105, 157–60, 169, 175, 184
Enlightenment, 55
Erdogan, Recep Tayyip, 51
Ethiopia, 83
ethnic identities, 16, 97, 101, 175–77
Eurasia Group, 38, 65, 114
Eurasian Question, 109
European Union (EU), 76, 121, 122, 149
existentialism, 159–60
exurbs, 140, 150

Facebook, 170
fascism, 5, 7, 140, 182
fatalism, 172
February Revolution, 30

Fight Between Carnival and Lent (Brueghel), 23
financial markets, 40–41, 122–23
Finland, 121–22
Florida, Richard, 132, 161–62
Floyd, George, 89, 140–42, 163, 171
"folk," 139–40, 148, 150–51, 160
Foreign Affairs, 53–54, 57, 62
Fox News, 145
France, 71, 84, 88, 97, 121–22, 172
Franco-Prussian War, 24, 79
Frederick II (the Great), 100
Freikorps, 9, 10
French Revolution, 24, 137, 163
Friedrich, Carl, 182–83
Frost, Robert, 157

Gaddafi, Muammar, 44–45
Ganesh, Janan, 62
Garfield, James, 135
gas, Russian, 96–97, 119
Gaza War, 39, 52, 54, 55, 79, 81, 84, 89, 124–26
  Biden administration and, 49
  smart bombs use, 46–47
Gazprom, 96
Gehry, Frank, 132
"Geographical Pivot of History, The" (Mackinder), 37–38
geography, shrinkage of, 34–37, 52
George Floyd protests, 89, 140–42, 163, 171
Germany. *See also* Nazi Germany
  NATO and Russia, 121–22
  Weimar Republic, 3–5, 7–14, 16–17, 19, 33, 35, 52–53, 70, 186
"Gerontion" (Eliot), 159
glasnost, 74–75
globalization, 6–7, 56, 63, 85–90
Globalization 1.0, 85–88
Globalization 2.0, 85, 88–90
global warming. *See* climate change

200

INDEX

Global War on Terrorism, 55, 77–78, 99, 124
Goethe, Johann Wolfgang von, 36
Goodbye to Berlin (Isherwood), 3–4
Google, 138, 173
Gorbachev, Mikhail, 74–76, 91, 112, 113
Gore, Al, 76
Gray, Colin S., 43, 55–57, 78
"Great Blight of Dullness," 130–31, 133
Great Britain, 16, 18, 71, 73, 104, 116, 121
Great Depression, 8–9, 35–36
Great Illusion, The (Angell), 54
great-power decline, 119–21
great-power rivalries, 55–56, 77, 79
Great Recession, 9
Greco-Turkish War, 120
Greece, 35, 121
Greece, ancient, 35, 145–46, 181
Green, Dominic, 137
groupthink, 138, 144, 154, 163
Grygiel, Jakub, 81
Guggenheim, Peggy, 156–57
gulags, 19, 100–101
Gulf War, 41, 46
Guns of August, The (Tuchman), 71
Guterres, António, 84
G-Zero, 38

Habsburgs, 14–15, 36, 152
hacking, 42–43, 55, 117
Hamas, 46–47, 78, 82, 89, 125–27, 161
Hammarskjöld, Dag, 84
Hand, Learned, 184
Harrison, Benjamin, 135
Harvest of Sorrow, The (Conquest), 72
Hayward, Max, 164
Herzen, Alexander, 183–84
Herzl, Theodore, 176

Hesse, Hermann, 5
Hezbollah, 125
hierarchy, 19, 27
Hindenburg, Paul von, 13
Hitler, Adolf, 50, 51, 54, 134, 139, 174, 176, 185
  Beer Hall Putsch, 10–12
  Churchill on, 14–15
  rise to power, 4, 7, 10–14, 16, 17, 36, 98, 152
  during World War II, 55, 79–80, 96, 108, 167
Hobbes, Thomas, 16, 66, 123
Hohenzollerns, 14–15, 17, 32, 152
Holocaust, 54, 55, 126–27, 160
Holodomor, 72
Hong Kong, 89
Hu Jintao, 113–15
humanitarianism, 77
human nature, 16, 50–55
human rights, 18–19
Hungary, 51, 74, 97
"hunting pack," 166–67, 170
Huntington, Samuel, 17, 64, 124, 172
Hussein, Saddam, 31
Huttenlocher, Daniel, 173–74
Huxley, Aldous, 168–69
hydrogen bombs, 36, 44, 50

Ibn Khaldun, Abd al-Rahman, 147–49, 151
ideology, 137, 180
immigration, 58, 153
imperial decline, 119–21
imperialism, 15, 153
India, 44, 82–83, 94, 116, 146
Indochina, 104
Industrial Revolution, 56, 75, 132, 171
inequality, 130–32
inflation, 3–5, 8–9, 26, 40, 76, 167
interconnectedness, 6–7, 14, 38–42

INDEX

Iran, 104, 125–28
  anti-government demonstrations, 127–28, 171–72
  social media and, 146, 171–72, 175
Iranian Revolution, 31–32, 104, 128, 163
Iraq, 31, 106
Iraq War, 35, 55, 66, 77–78, 80, 87, 90–93, 108
Isherwood, Christopher, 3–4, 11
Islamic terrorism, 46, 77–78, 87–88
isolationism, 128
Israel
  anti-Semitism, 83, 124–27
  Hamas attack on, 46–47, 78, 82, 89, 125–27, 161
  Hezbollah and, 125
  Sunni Arab alliance, 82
  United Nations and, 83–84
Italian Renaissance, 147

Jacobs, Jane, 130–34, 150, 161, 186
James, Henry, 160
Japan, 41, 52, 77, 111, 116, 117, 123, 126
Jiang Zemin, 115
John Paul II, Pope, 74
Johnson, Lyndon, 93
Jordan, 125
Joyce, James, 160
Judd, Dennis R., 131
July 14 Revolution, 31

Kant, Immanuel, 86, 87, 134
Kazakhstan, 19
Kennedy, John F., 93
Kerensky, Alexander, 30, 31
Khamenei, Ali, 125
Khomeini, Ruhollah, 32
Khrushchev, Nikita, 33, 83, 124–25
Kim Jong-un, 45

Kirkpatrick, Jeane J., 103–5, 108
Kissinger, Henry, 16, 32, 44, 50–51, 173–74
Klimt, Gustav, 176
Kokoschka, Oskar, 176
Koolhaas, Rem, 133
Korean War, 48–49
Kosovo War, 77, 84–85
Kotkin, Joel, 132, 134
Krisenbilder, 39–40
Kristallnacht, 163
Kuwait, 106

Länder, 8–9
Laqueur, Walter, 182
Last Train to Zona Verde, The (Theroux), 61–62
Lebanon, 125
Lenin, Vladimir, 23, 28–30, 31, 32, 72, 100, 102, 103, 106–7, 113, 134, 141
Le Pen, Marine, 97
liberal arts education, 107, 154
liberalism, 176, 183–85
Liberian War, 66
Libya, 44–45, 58, 66
linear thinking, 79
literary modernism, 159–60
"little green men," 99
logistics, 99, 101
London, 131, 158–59
loneliness, 142, 165–66, 173
"Love Song of J. Alfred Prufrock, The" (Eliot), 159
Lowell, Robert, 131
Lueger, Karl, 176

MacAskill, William, 185
McCarthy, Joseph, 168
Mackinder, Halford, 37–38
McKinley, William, 135
Magna Carta, 104
Mahoney, Daniel J., 28, 30

INDEX

Malthus, Thomas Robert, 60–61, 163
Manet, Édouard, 155
Mann, Golo, 8, 10, 13
Mann, Thomas, 5, 8
Mao Zedong, 34, 54, 114, 115, 124, 125, 134, 168, 171, 174
  Cultural Revolution, 110–11, 163
March 1917 (Solzhenitsyn), 20, 30
Marx, Karl, 113, 118, 134, 175
mass men, 178–81
mass shootings, 56, 178
Matsu Islands, 48–49
media, 7, 49–50, 79, 92, 93, 126, 142–47, 170. *See also* social media
Mein Kampf (Hitler), 11
Mendelssohn, Felix, 155
Merkel, Angela, 97
Mexico City, 129
Mexico-U.S. border, 58, 94
Middle East, 40, 87, 90, 123
  Arab Spring, 66, 171, 181
  modernizing dictatorships, 18
  population, 122
  resource scarcity, 67
  terrorism, 55, 78
Mikhail Aleksandrovich of Russia, 31
Mill, John Stuart, 184
Mitford, Nancy, 100
mobs, 28, 139–44, 146–47, 161, 164, 173–74
  social media and digital, 136, 142–44, 161, 170–71
modernism, 24, 33, 53–54, 66–67, 133, 159–60, 175
monarchy, 14–15, 17–19, 31–33
money culture, 152–53
Mongols, 53
"monotony," 130
Monsoon (Kaplan), 193*n*
Morocco, 147

Morson, Gary Saul, 141
Moynihan, Daniel Patrick, 83, 108
Muqaddimah (Ibn Khaldun), 147–49, 151
music, 155, 157, 177
Myers, Steven Lee, 76

Nagorno-Karabakh Armenians, 84
Napoleon Bonaparte, 16, 50, 51
Napoleonic Wars, 23, 70–71, 122
nationalism, 11, 111, 121, 136, 137, 185
NATO (North Atlantic Treaty Organization), 38, 51, 76–77, 95, 97–98, 105, 106, 116, 121–22
Nazi Germany (Nazism), 137, 141, 164
  anti-Semitism and Holocaust, 54, 55, 126–27, 145, 160, 167
  Beer Hall Putsch, 10–12
  rise to power, 10–14, 16, 17, 27, 167
  during World War II, 72–73, 79–80, 95–96, 108, 144–45
neoconservatism, 104, 183
New York City, 129, 148–49, 153
New York Times, The, 76, 135, 136, 142–45, 151, 161, 170–71
Nicaragua, 104
Nicholas II, 19, 21, 22, 30–31
Niebuhr, Reinhold, 18
Nietzsche, Friedrich, 178
Nigeria, 58, 66, 172
Nigerian coup d'état of 2023, 34
Nikolaevich, Nicholas, 31
Nineteen Eighty-Four (Orwell), 168–69
Nixon, Richard, 93, 125
Nobel Prize, 8, 20, 165
No Exit (Sartre), 6–7
nomads (nomadism), 147–48
noncommissioned officers (NCOs), 99

INDEX

Nord Stream AG, 96
North Africa, 147, 171
North Korea, 33, 45, 48–49, 116, 123–25, 127–28
nostalgia, 140
November 1916 (Solzhenitsyn), 20, 28–30
nuclear weapons, 39, 42, 43–50, 82–83, 114, 115–16, 120, 146
Nuclear Weapons and Foreign Policy (Kissinger), 50–51

October Revolution, 30
Oedipus Rex (Sophocles), 128
Oklahoma! (musical), 155
One Day in the Life of Ivan Denisovich (Solzhenitsyn), 100–101
On the Principle of Population (Malthus), 60–61
optimism, 12, 43, 53–54
Orbán, Viktor, 51, 97
order, 10, 16, 21, 27, 28, 81, 126, 153
Origins of Totalitarianism, The (Arendt), 142
Ortega y Gasset, José, 178–80
Orwell, George, 168–69
Ostpolitik, 96
Ottoman Empire, 15, 81, 107, 108–9, 120

"pack, the," 166–67
Pahlavi, Mohammed Reza, 31–32, 104, 128
Painted Word, The (Wolfe), 156
painting, 155–57
Pakistan, 44, 45, 82–83, 123, 146
Pale of Settlement, 126
Paris Peace Treaty (1919), 15
Parker, James, 158
Patapievici, Horia-Roman, 138
Peking University, 134
perestroika, 74–75
pessimism, 23, 43, 60, 62–64, 185–86

Peters, Ralph, 57
Philippine War, 117
phishing, 55
Pinker, Steven, 53–56
"pivot" theory, 37–38
Plutarch, 110
Poland, 73, 74, 121
political polarization, 145, 148–49
Pol Pot, 32
population, 60, 67–68, 118, 122, 123–24, 161, 172
pornography, 55
postmodernism, 124, 135, 152, 159, 181–82
Pound, Ezra, 159
poverty, 39, 43, 63, 68, 74, 86, 132, 177
precision-guided weaponry, 45–47, 82, 105, 146
premonitions, 4–5, 23
presentness, 86
presidential campaigns, 135
press. *See* media
"progress," 164, 175
Prunier, Gérard, 66–67
Prussia, 8, 15, 22, 24, 79, 100
public executions, 166–67
Putin, Vladimir, 33, 34, 45, 52, 76, 78, 79–80, 87–88, 95, 102, 125, 174
 decline of Russia, 105–9, 120–21
 Ukraine War, 27, 44, 45, 48, 50, 51, 79, 98–99, 105–9, 125

Qing dynasty, 119
Quemoy Island, 48–49

railways, 37, 126
Rathenau, Walther, 10
rationalism, 55
Reagan, Ronald, 74, 93, 104
realism, 54, 71
reason, 21–22

Rebel, The (Camus), 181
Reconstruction of Nations, The (Snyder), 139–40
Red Wheel series of Solzhenitsyn, 19–32
Reed, John, 30
Reign of Terror, 24
remote work, 180
resource scarcity, 63–64, 67, 123
Return of Marco Polo's World, The (Kaplan), 119
Revenge of Geography, The (Kaplan), 119, 126
Revolt of the Masses, The (Ortega), 179
Revolutions of 1848, 183, 185
righteousness, 32, 50
Rilke, Rainer Maria, 5, 158
Rite of Spring, The (Stravinsky), 157
Rodgers and Hammerstein, 155
Roman Colosseum, 139
Romania, 26, 74, 121, 164, 165
Romanovs, 15–16, 23, 31, 32, 71, 118
Roosevelt, Franklin D., 109
Rosneft, 96
Rudd, Kevin, 115
rumors, 135–36
Russia, 70–80, 87–88, 90–91, 94, 125. *See also* Putin, Vladimir; Soviet Union; Ukraine War
connectedness, 7
decline of, 95–103, 105–9, 119, 120–22, 128
modernizing dictatorship of, 18, 19, 108
Solzhenitsyn on, 19–32
Ukraine occupation of 2014, 51, 79–80, 97, 105
Russian Revolution, 19–22, 30–31, 72, 141, 152, 163

Rwandan Genocide, 66
Rybczynski, Witold, 132

Saint-Saëns, Camille, 155
Sanders, Bernie, 20
Sartre, Jean-Paul, 6–7, 134, 159–60
Saudi Arabia, 82
Schmidt, Eric, 173–74
Schönberg, Arnold, 5
Schönerer, Georg von, 176
Schorske, Carl E., 176–77
Schröder, Gerhard, 96–97
Schubert, Franz, 155
Schumann, Robert, 155
Schwartz, Delmore, 159
Scruton, Roger, 133–34, 151–52, 161
Second Amendment, 140
Semafor, 143
September 11 attacks (2001), 55, 77–78, 87–88
Shakespeare, William, 13, 64
Shakespearean decline, 91, 129
shantih, 158–59
"shock therapy," 75, 111
Siberia, 82, 96, 101, 106, 128
Sicilian Expedition, 35–36
Sierra Leone Civil War, 65–66
Silicon Valley, 86
Six-Day War, 83
smart bombs, 46–47
Smith, Adam, 60
Snyder, Timothy, 53–54, 139–40
social control, 181
social media, 49, 93, 142, 146
cities and, 129–32, 136
crowds and, 170, 172, 174–75
Solzhenitsyn, Aleksandr, 19–32, 71, 100–101, 135, 152, 164
August 1914, 20, 23–28
November 1916, 20, 28–30
Somoza, Anastasio, 104
Sondheim, Stephen, 155
Sophocles, 155

INDEX

South Africa, 61–62, 172
South Korea, 32, 48–49, 123, 127–28
South Ossetia, 79, 98
"Soviet bloc," 73–74, 96
Soviet Union, 10, 33, 41, 42, 44, 72–76, 124–25, 149. *See also* Cold War; Russia
   Afghanistan invasion, 101–2, 125
   collapse of, 20, 74–76, 98, 102, 113, 118, 125
   gulags, 19, 100–101
   U.N. Security Council and, 84
   during World War II, 72–73, 84, 95–96, 100, 108
Spanish-American War, 94–95
specialization, 154, 168, 178–79
Spengler, Oswald, 139–40, 144–58, 165, 169, 175, 177
Stalin, Joseph, 19, 73, 74, 100–102, 108, 113, 124, 171, 174
Stalinism, 33, 102, 137, 141, 165
status quo, 50–51
Stearns, Jason K., 57–58, 62
Sternhell, Zeev, 182
stock markets, 4, 40, 86
Stolypin, Pyotr, 22, 26, 31
Stratfor, 65
Strausz-Hupé, Robert, 180, 185
Stravinsky, Igor, 155, 157
Streicher, Julius, 145
Stresemann, Gustav, 12, 35
style, 150–51, 154–55, 174, 177
Styron, William, 148
suburbs, 136, 138, 140, 149–50, 161–62
Sudan, 58
Sudetenland, 79–80
Sulzberger, A. G., 143
supply chains, 40, 42, 59, 89, 99
Swanstrom, Todd, 131
Sweden, 121–22
Syria, 51, 66, 70, 79, 98

Taiwan, 39, 41–42, 48–49, 82, 89, 91, 116, 119
technology, 6, 32–34, 38, 48, 52, 57, 78, 138, 142. *See also* artificial intelligence
   financial markets and, 40
   war and weapons, 42–43, 50, 57
temperate zone, 38
Ten Days That Shook the World (Reed), 30
terrorism, 46, 77–78, 87–88
Theroux, Paul, 61–62
think tanks, 152–53
Thucydides, 35, 36
Tiananmen Square protests, 112
Tokyo, 129
Tooze, Adam, 39–40
totalitarianism, 5, 14, 33, 115, 168–69, 182–83
Transformation of War, The (Van Creveld), 57, 58
Treaty of Rapallo, 10
Treaty of Versailles, 9, 10, 12, 14
tribalism, 64, 66, 177
Trillin, Calvin, 148
Trotsky, Leon, 30
Truman, Harry, 93
Trump, Donald, 17, 34, 49, 89, 92–94, 136, 140
Tuchman, Barbara, 71
Turkey, 51, 63, 88, 108–9, 120, 121
Tuva, 128
tyranny, 12, 13, 34, 165, 172, 174
tyranny of the crowd, 167–71

Ukraine, Russian occupation of 2014, 51, 79–80, 97, 105
Ukraine War, 27, 38–42, 48, 50, 51, 54, 55, 70, 79, 89–90, 105–9
   Biden administration and, 49, 80
   interconnectedness and, 38–42, 52
   nuclear weapons threat, 44, 45

INDEX

Russia decline and, 80–82, 92, 98–99, 101–2, 105–9, 128
   Solzhenitsyn and, 23, 25, 27
   United Nations and, 84
Under Western Eyes (Conrad), 29
United Nations (U.N.), 38, 61, 82, 83–85
   Human Development Index, 123
   Security Council, 84
urbanization, 59, 61, 105, 129–37, 161–62. *See also* cities
urban riots, 163–64
   George Floyd protests, 89, 140–42, 163, 171
U Thant, 84

van Creveld, Martin, 57, 58
Vietnam, 94
Vietnam War, 35, 46, 49, 76, 80, 93, 95, 117
Vogel, Ezra, 110–12
Voltaire, 36
von Neumann, John, 36–38, 89
von Papen, Franz, 13, 17, 34

Wagner Group, 99, 125
Waldheim, Kurt, 84
Wall Street Journal, The, 173
Warhol, Andy, 148
Warsaw Pact, 74–76
"Was Democracy Just a Moment?" (Kaplan), 65
Washington, D.C., 69–70
Waste Land, The (Eliot), 105, 158–60, 169, 175
waste lands, 162–63

Wat, Aleksander, 137–38
Wealth of Nations, The (Smith), 60
weapons of mass destruction, 44–45, 66
Weimar Republic, 3–5, 7–14, 16–17, 19, 33, 35, 52–53, 70, 186
Wemple, Erik, 143–44
West Side Story (musical), 155
Wilhelm II, 8
Wilson, Edmund, 131
Wittelsbachs, 14–15, 17
Wolfe, Tom, 156
world-city, 139, 150–51, 155, 172
world poverty, 39, 43, 63, 68, 74, 86, 132, 177
World Restored, A (Kissinger), 32
World War I, 8, 9, 15, 38, 54, 71–72, 95, 106–7, 120, 158, 170, 185
   Solzhenitsyn's *August 1914,* 20, 23–28
World War II, 14, 16, 70, 72–73, 100, 108, 116, 144–45, 160, 170
   Battle of Stalingrad, 73, 95–96
   bombing during, 45, 46, 77
   Pinker on, 53, 54
   Solzhenitsyn and, 19

Xi Jinping, 34, 52, 78, 91, 107–8, 111–15, 117–18, 127, 174

Yeltsin, Boris, 76, 87–88, 102, 105
Yemen, 66
youth, worship of, 58, 110, 151–52
Yugoslavia, 80–81, 120

Zelenskyy, Volodymyr, 81

ABOUT THE AUTHOR

ROBERT D. KAPLAN is the bestselling author of twenty-three books on foreign affairs and travel, including *The Loom of Time, Adriatic, The Good American, The Revenge of Geography, Asia's Cauldron, Monsoon, The Coming Anarchy,* and *Balkan Ghosts,* which have been translated into many languages. He holds the Robert Strausz-Hupé Chair in Geopolitics at the Foreign Policy Research Institute. For three decades he reported on foreign affairs for *The Atlantic.* He was a member of the Pentagon's Defense Policy Board and the Chief of Naval Operations Executive Panel. *Foreign Policy* twice named him one of the world's Top 100 Global Thinkers.

robertdkaplan.com

ABOUT THE TYPE

This book was set in Bembo, a typeface based on an oldstyle Roman face that was used for Cardinal Pietro Bembo's tract *De Aetna* in 1495. Bembo was cut by Francesco Griffo (1450–1518) in the early sixteenth century for Italian Renaissance printer and publisher Aldus Manutius (1449–1515). The Lanston Monotype Company of Philadelphia brought the well-proportioned letterforms of Bembo to the United States in the 1930s.